ORDNAN

GW00402901

Cycle

TOURS

22 one-day routes

Around Birmingham

Compiled by
Mike Ginger, Rob Green
and Gordon Selway

HAMLYN

Contents

Routes

Acknowledgements

AA Photo Library 43, 53, 64, 89, 95 bottom, 107 bottom, 113 • WM Chambers 19, 23, 77, 83, 101; Heart of England Tourist Board 125 • Judy Todd back cover, 47, 95 top, 107 top, 137

Back cover photograph: Stepping stones at Cannock Chase

First published 1995 by

Ordnance Survey and Hamlyn, an imprint of
Romsey Road   Reed Books
Maybush   Michelin House
Southampton   81 Fulham Road
SO16 4GU   London SW3 6RB

Text and compilation
Copyright © Reed International Books Ltd 1995
Maps Copyright © Crown Copyright 1995
First edition 1995

A catalogue record for this atlas is available from the British Library

ISBN 0 600 58623 5
(Ordnance Survey ISBN 0 319 00772 3)

Made, printed and published in Great Britain

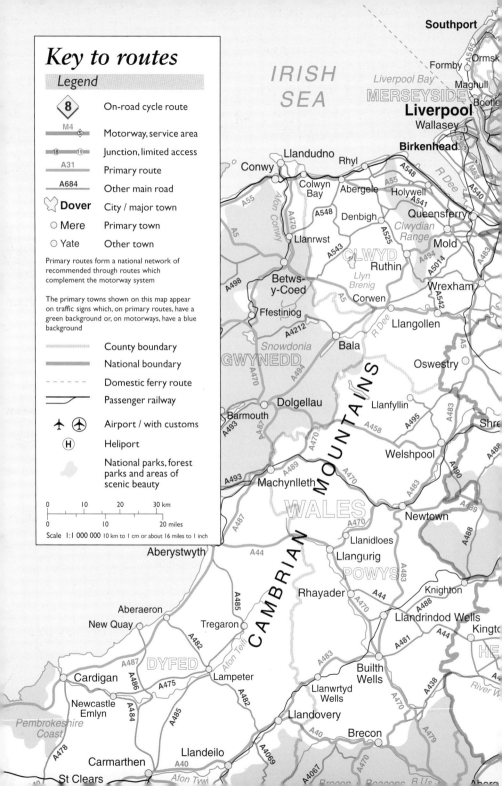

Key to routes

Legend

8   On-road cycle route

M4   Ⓢ   Motorway, service area

18   19   Junction, limited access

A31   Primary route

A684   Other main road

⬦ **Dover**   City / major town

○ Mere   Primary town

○ Yate   Other town

Primary routes form a national network of recommended through routes which complement the motorway system

The primary towns shown on this map appear on traffic signs which, on primary routes, have a green background or, on motorways, have a blue background

╌╌╌╌ County boundary

━━━ National boundary

╌ ╌ ╌ Domestic ferry route

━━━ Passenger railway

✈ Ⓐ Airport / with customs

Ⓗ Heliport

National parks, forest parks and areas of scenic beauty

Scale 1:1 000 000 10 km to 1 cm or about 16 miles to 1 inch

0   10   20   30 km
0   10   20 miles

IRISH SEA

Southport

Formby   Ormsk

Liverpool Bay   Maghull

MERSEYSIDE   Bootle

Liverpool

Wallasey

Birkenhead

Llandudno   Rhyl

Conwy   Colwyn Bay   Abergele   Holywell

Denbigh   Queensferry

Llanrwst   Clwydian Range

CLWYD

Ruthin   Mold

Llyn Brenig

Betws-y-Coed   Corwen   Wrexham

Ffestiniog   Langollen

R Dee   Oswestry

Bala

Snowdonia   GWYNEDD   Llanfyllin

Dolgellau

Barmouth   Welshpool

CAMBRIAN MOUNTAINS

Machynlleth

WALES   Newtown

Llanidloes

Aberystwyth   Llangurig

POWYS

Rhayader   Knighton

Aberaeron   Tregaron   Llandrindod Wells

New Quay   Kingto

DYFED   Builth Wells

Cardigan   Lampeter   Llanwrtyd Wells

Newcastle Emlyn   Llandovery

River W

Carmarthen   Llandeilo   Brecon

St Clears   Afon Tywi

Quick reference chart

Route	Page	Distance (miles)	Grade (easy/moderate/strenuous)	Links with other routes[1]	Tourist information centres[2]
1 From Lichfield along country lanes towards Cannock Chase through Fradley and Farewell	18	20	◆◆	2, 21	Lichfield 01543-252109
2 From Lichfield east through the villages of south Derbyshire and the Trent Valley	22	25	◆◆	1	Lichfield 01543-252109
3 From Chester Road into easy countryside northeast of Birmingham visiting Kingsbury Water Park	26	20	◆		Birmingham 0121-643 2514
4 From Nuneaton to the birthplace of modern England	30	30	◆◆		Nuneaton 01203-384027
5 From Coventry visiting the diverse villages of the green belt between Birmingham and Coventry	36	36	◆◆◆	6	Coventry 01203-832303
6 From Dorridge past medieval houses and through relics of the Forest of Arden to a romantic ruined castle	42	31	◆	5, 8	Kenilworth 01926-52595
7 From Leamington to Charlecote Park and the historic town of Warwick	46	47	◆◆		Leamington Spa 01926-311470
8 From Dorridge to Stratford-upon-Avon returning via Wilmcote	52	43	◆◆	6	Stratford-upon-Avon 01789-293127
9 From Yardley Wood station to the village of Tanworth, returning by ancient sunken lanes	58	22	◆◆	10, 11	Solihull 0121-704 6130
10 From Redditch to the relics of a medieval forest and through the Arrow valley	64	36	◆◆	9, 11	Redditch 01527-60806
11 From King's Norton across valley heads to Huddington	70	55	◆◆◆	9, 10, 13, 14	Bromsgrove 01527-831809
12 From Droitwich to Great Witley and back down the wonderful Teme Valley	76	37	◆◆◆◆	GHW3	Malvern 01684-892289

| --- | --- | --- | --- | --- | --- |
13 From Longbridge across the Lickey Hills to Dodford and the Clent Hills	82	35	🚲🚲🚲🚲	11, 14	Bromsgrove 01527-831809
14 From Longbridge by winding country lanes to old centres of agricultural industry and ancient woods	88	32	🚲🚲🚲	11, 13	Bromsgrove 01527-831809
15 From Stourbridge to a sandstone outcrop, and a river-powered ferry	94	45	🚲🚲🚲🚲	16	Bewdley 01299-404740
16 From Wolverhampton across undulating country to dramatic vistas in the Severn Valley	100	55	🚲🚲🚲	15, 17, 18	Bridgnorth 01746-763358
17 From Wolverhampton to the cradle of the Industrial Revolution	106	42	🚲🚲🚲	16, 18	Wolverhampton 01902-312051
18 From Wolverhampton to Charles II's hiding place through intriguing villages and 18th-century	112	30	🚲	16, 17	Wolverhampton 01902-312051
19 From Stafford to Butter Hill, along the Shropshire Union Canal to High Offley then Eccleshall	118	30	🚲🚲	20	Stafford 01785-40204
20 From Stafford through ancient Abbots Bromley returning via Cannock Chase or Shugborough Hall	124	43	🚲🚲	19, 21	Stafford 01785-40204
21 From Great Wyrley through old mining areas, across upland heaths and forests	130	25	🚲🚲🚲🚲	1, 20	Lichfield 01543-252109
22 From Burton across Needwood to Uttoxeter, returning along the Dove Valley	136	40	🚲🚲		Burton-on-Trent 01283-516609

Distances are for the full route. Many rides also have shorter routes, which may have an easier grading as well.

[1]**Links with other rides** Use this information to vary the start of some rides, to create a more strenuous ride, or if you are planning to do more than one ride in a day, or on a weekend or over a few days. The rides do not necessarily join up: there may be a gap of up to five miles between the closest points or the best route to link the rides. The routes form an informal and largely interconnected network around the West Midlands conurbation, and may be used

as the basis for longer cycling tours and for routes into other areas. GHW3 is on-road route 3 in OS Cycle Tours, Gloucestershire, Hereford and Worcester

[2]**Tourist Information Centres** You can contact them for information about places of interest on the rides, or for details of accommodation if you are using the routes to work out a cycling tour. If they cannot help, there are many books recommending places to stay. If nothing is listed for the place where you want to stay, try phoning the village post office or pub to see if they can

Around Birmingham

*T*he routes in this book take you into the Heart of England – the green belt which surrounds the West Midlands conurbation and the countryside beyond – within a radius of about 30 to 40 miles from Birmingham.

Birmingham was one of many small settlements recorded in 1086 by Domesday, remote from the main centres and routes in the woodland of its relatively infertile plateau. Over the centuries the mineral wealth of the Black Country, the coal and the limestone in particular, was exploited in basic industries; Birmingham, away from the minerals but at the meeting point of many minor tracks, grew into a manufacturing and commercial centre.

North and east of the city the land falls away gradually along the Tame Valley towards the Trent. Here there is much open country, explored in the rides centred on Lichfield, and in the rides from Coventry and Nuneaton, which also visit the uplands of Warwickshire, the former Forest of Arden and undulating west Leicestershire.

To the southeast, rides from Dorridge, Yardley Wood, Leamington and Redditch also take you into Arden and into the open, rich argicultural areas of the Avon Valley and the Warwickshire Feldon.

The routes from Longbridge and Kings Norton wind over the Clent and Lickey Hills into the Severn basin where little streams have carved narrow valleys in the Clent Hills to then flow through broader dales.

Shropshire and Staffordshire offer further variety. West of Stafford there is the cradle of the Industrial Revolution at Ironbridge, while upland heath and woodland are visited on the rides to Abbots Bromley, around Cannock Chase and through Needwood.

Preface

Several routes are based on those in the West Midlands Bicycle Rides leaflets. We would like to thank all the people who assisted in preparing the text, rode many of the routes, and made helpful suggestions: Steve Ancell, Chris Crean, Tattwa Gyani, John Newson, Barbie Norden, Sally Robinson, Dave Thompson, John Tozer. Please let us know how you find the rides. We can be contacted via the publishers

Abbreviations and instructions

Instructions are given as concisely as possible to make them easy to follow while you are cycling. Remember to read one or two instructions ahead so that you do not miss a turning. This is most likely to occur when you have to turn off a road on which you have been riding for a fairly long distance and these junctions are marked **Easy to miss** to warn you.

If there appears to be a contradiction between the instructions and what you actually see, always refer to the map. There are many reasons why over the course of a few years instructions will need updating as new roads are built and priorities and signposts change.

If giving instructions for road routes is at times difficult, doing so for off-road routes can often be almost impossible, particularly when the route passes through woodland. With few signposts and buildings to orientate yourself by, more attention is paid to other features, such as gradient and surface. Most rides were explored between late spring and early autumn; the countryside changes dramatically in winter. If in doubt, consult your map and compass to see that you are heading in the right direction.

Mud is mentioned where it was encountered on the exploration, or where we are particularly aware that it may be a problem. The situation may however change, not only from summer to winter, but also from dry to wet weather at any time during the year. At times you may have to retrace your steps and find an on-road alternative.

Some routes have small sections that follow footpaths. The instructions will highlight these sections where you must get off and push your bike. You may only ride on bridleways and by-ways so be careful if you stray from the given routes.

Directions

L	left
LH	left-hand
RH	right-hand
SA	straight ahead or straight across
bear L or R	make less than a 90-degree (right-angle) turn at a fork in the road or track or at a sharp bend so that your course appears to be straight ahead; this is often written as *in effect SA*
sharp L or R turn	is more acute than 90 degrees
sharp R/L back on yourself	an almost U-turn
sharp LH/RH bend	a 90-degree bend
R then L or R	the second turning is visible then immediately L from the first
R then 1st L	the second turning may be some distance from the first; the distance may also be indicated: *R, then after 1 mile L*

Junctions

T-j	T-junction, a junction where you have to give way
X-roads	crossroads, a junction where you may or may not have to give way
offset X-roads	the four roads are not in the form of a perfect cross and you will have to turn left then right, or vice versa, to continue the route

Signs

'Placename 2'	words in quotation marks are those that appear on signposts; the numbers indicate distance in miles unless stated otherwise
NS	not signposted
trig point	a trigonometrical station

Instructions

An example of an easy instruction is:

4 At the T-j at the end of Smith Road by the White Swan PH R on Brown Street 'Greentown 2, Redville 3'.

There is more information in this instruction than you would normally need, but things do change: pubs may close down and signs may be replaced, removed or vandalized.

An example of a difficult instruction is:

8 Shortly after the brow of the hill, soon after passing a telephone box on the right next L (NS).

As you can see, there is no T-junction to halt you in your tracks, no signpost indicating where the left turn will take you, so you need to have your wits about you in order not to miss the turning.

Fact boxes

The introduction to each route includes a fact box giving useful information:

Start

This is the suggested start point coinciding with instruction 1 on the map.

Distance and grade

The distance is, of course, that from the beginning to the end of the route.

The number of drinks bottles indicates the grade:

Easy

Moderate

Strenuous

The grade is based on the amount of climbing involved rather than the distance covered. Remember that conditions may vary dramatically with the weather and seasons

Page diagrams

The page diagrams on the introductory pages of a route show how the following map pages have cover the route, how they overlap and if any inset maps have been used

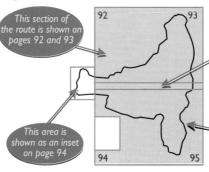

Terrain

This brief description of the terrain may be read in conjunction with the cross-profile diagram at the foot of the page to help you to plan your journey

Nearest railway

The stations listed are either on or near the route but not necessarily at the start.

The train symbols indicate the approximate level of service to be expected:

🚂 *Frequent, year-round*
🚂 *Limited or seasonal*

The signal symbols indicate how bicycle-friendly these services are likely to be:

🚦 *Generally few or no restrictions*
🚦 *Bicycles usually only carried in limited numbers, reservations may be necessary and a fee may be charged*

You are strongly advised to check with British Rail or the appropriate train operating company for specific details when planning to travel (see page 15)

Before you go

Preparing yourself

Fitness

🔹 Cycling uses muscles in a different way from walking or running, so if you are beginning or returning to it after a long absence you will need time to train your muscles and become accustomed to sitting on a saddle for a few hours. Build up your fitness and stamina gradually and make sure you are using a bicycle that is the right size for you and suits your needs.

Equipment

🔹 Attach the following items to the bike: bell, pump, light-brackets and lights, lock-holder and lock, rack and panniers or elastic straps for securing things to the rack, map holder. Unless it is the middle of summer and the weather is guaranteed to be fine, you will need to carry extra clothes, particularly a waterproof, with you, and it is well worth investing in a rack for this purpose.

🔹 Wearing a small pouch around your waist is the easiest and safest way of carrying small tools and personal equipment. The basics are: Allen keys to fit the various Allen bolts on your bike, chainlink extractor, puncture repair kit, reversible screwdriver (slot and crosshead), small adjustable spanner, spare inner tube, tyre levers (not always necessary with mountain bike tyres), coins and a phonecard for food and telephone calls, compass.

🔹 Additional tools for extended touring: bottom bracket extractor, cone spanners, freewheel extractor, headset spanners, lubricant, socket spanner for pedals, spare cables, spoke-key.

Clothing

🔹 What you wear when you are cycling should be comfortable, allowing you, and most especially your legs, to move freely. It should also be practical, so that it will keep you warm and dry if and when the weather changes.

🔹 *Feet* You can cycle in just about any sort of footwear, but bear in mind that the chain has oil on it, so do not use your very best shoes. Leather tennis shoes or something similar, with a smooth sole to slip into the pedal and toe clip are probably adequate until you buy specialist cycling shoes, which have stiffer soles and are sometimes designed for use with specialist pedals.

🔹 *Legs* Cycling shorts or padded cycling underwear worn under everyday clothing make long rides much more comfortable. Avoid tight, non-stretch trousers, which are very uncomfortable for cycling and will sap your energy, as they restrict the movement of your legs; baggy tracksuit

11

bottoms, which can get caught in the chain and will sag around your ankles if they get wet. Almost anything else will do, though a pair of stretch leggings is probably best.

- **Upper body** What you wear should be long enough to cover your lower back when you are leaning forward and, ideally, should have zips or buttons that you can adjust to regulate your temperature. Several thin layers are better than one thick layer.

- **Head** A helmet may protect your head in a fall.

- **Wet weather** If you get soaked to your skin and you are tired, your body core temperature can drop very quickly when you are cycling. A waterproof, windproof top is essential if it looks like rain. A dustbin bag would be better than nothing but obviously a breathable waterproof material is best.

- **Cold weather** Your extremities suffer far more when you are cycling than when you are walking in similar conditions. A hat that covers your ears, a scarf around your neck, a pair of warm gloves and a thermal top and bottom combined with what you would normally wear cycling should cover almost all conditions.

- **Night and poor light** Wearing light-coloured clothes or reflective strips is almost as important as having lights on your bike. Reflective bands worn around the ankles are particularly effective in making you visible to motorists.

Preparing your bicycle

- You may not be a bicycle maintenance expert, but you should make sure that your bike is roadworthy before you begin a ride.

- If you are planning to ride in soft, off-road conditions, fit fat, knobbly tyres. If you are using the bike around town or on a road route, fit narrower, smoother tyres.

- Check the tyres for punctures or damage and repair or replace if necessary or if you are in any doubt. Keep tyres inflated hard (recommended pressures are on the side wall of the tyre) for mainly on-road riding. You do not need to inflate tyres as hard for off-road use; slightly softer tyres give some cushioning and get better traction in muddy conditions.

- Ensure that the brakes work efficiently. Replace worn cables and brake blocks.

- The bike should glide along silently. Tighten and adjust any part that is loose or rubbing against a moving part. Using a good-quality bike oil lubricate the hubs, bottom bracket, pedals where they join the cranks, chain and gear-changing mechanism from both sides. If the bike still makes grating noises, replace the bearings.

- Adjust the saddle properly. You can raise or lower it, move it forwards or backwards or tilt it up or down. The saddle height should ensure that your legs are working efficiently: too low and your knees will ache; too high and your hips will be rocking in order for your feet to reach the pedals.

- Some women find the average bike saddle uncomfortable because the female pelvis is a different shape from the male pelvis and needs a broader saddle for support. Some manufacturers make saddles especially for women.

Cross-profiles

The introduction to each route includes a cross-profile diagram. The vertical scale is the same on each diagram but the horizontal scale varies according to the length of the route

Longbridge Start / finish Lickey Lydiate Ash Upper Catshill Dodford Cooksey Green Rushock

Tips for touring

England and Wales have 120 000 miles of rights of way, but under the Wildlife and Countryside Act of 1968 you are allowed to cycle on only about 10 percent of them, namely on bridleways, by-ways open to all traffic (BOATS) and roads used as public paths (RUPPS).

The other 90 percent of rights of way are footpaths, where you may walk and usually push your bike, but not ride it. Local bylaws sometimes prohibit the pushing of bicycles along footpaths and although all the paths in this book have been checked, bylaws do sometimes change.

- You are not allowed to ride where there is no right of way. If you lose the route and find yourself in conflict with a landowner, stay calm and courteous, make a note of exactly where you are and then contact the Rights of Way Department of the local authority. It has copies of definitive maps and will take up the matter on your behalf if you are in the right.

- For further information on cycling and the law contact the Cyclists Touring Club (CTC) whose address can be found on the inside back cover.

Cycling techniques

If you are not used to cycling more than a few miles at a stretch, you may find initially that touring is tiring. There are ways of conserving your energy, however:

- Do not struggle in a difficult gear if you have an easier one. Let the gears help you up the hills. No matter how many gears a bike has, however, ultimately it is leg power that you need to get you up a hill. You may decide to get off and walk uphill with your bike to rest your muscles.

- You can save a lot of energy on the road by following close behind a stronger rider in his or her slipstream, but do not try this offroad. All the routes are circular, so you can start at any point and follow the instructions until you return to it. This is useful when there is a strong wind, as you can alter the route to go into the wind at the start of the ride, when you are fresh, and have the wind behind you on the return, when you are more tired.

- The main difference in technique between on-road and off-road cycling lies in getting your weight balanced correctly. When going down steep off-road sections, lower the saddle, keep the pedals level, stand up out of the saddle to let your legs absorb the bumps and keep your weight over the rear wheel. Control is paramount: keep your eyes on what lies ahead.

Chaddesley Corbett

Hillpool

Drayton

Belbroughton

Clent

Rumbow Cottages

Start / finish

Traffic

The rides in this book are designed to minimize time spent on busy roads, but you will inevitably encounter some traffic. The most effective way to avoid an accident with a motor vehicle is to be highly aware of what is going on around you and to ensure that other road users are aware of you.

- Ride confidently.
- Indicate clearly to other road users what you intend to do, particularly when turning right. Look behind you, wait for a gap in the traffic, indicate, then turn. If you have to turn right off a busy road or on a difficult bend, pull in and wait for a gap in the traffic or go past the turning to where you have a clear view of the traffic in both directions, then cross and return to the turning.
- Use your lights and wear reflective clothing at night and in poor light.
- Do not ride two-abreast if there is a vehicle behind you. Let it pass. If it cannot easily overtake you because the road is narrow, look for a passing place or a gate entrance and pull in to let it pass.

Maintenance

Mountain bikes are generally stronger than road bikes, but any bike can suffer. To prevent damage as far as possible:

- Watch out for holes and obstacles.
- Clean off mud and lubricate moving parts regularly.
- Replace worn parts, particularly brake blocks.

Riders also need maintenance:

- Eat before you get hungry, drink before you get thirsty. Dried fruit, nuts and chocolate take up little space and provide lots of energy.
- Carry a water bottle and keep it filled, especially on hot days. Tea, water and well-diluted soft drinks are the best thirst-quenchers.

Breakdowns

The most likely breakdown to occur is a puncture.

- Always carry a pump.
- Take a spare inner tube so that you can leave the puncture repair until later.
- Make sure you know how to remove a wheel. This may require an adjustable spanner or, in many cases, no tool at all, as many bikes now have wheels with quick-release skewers that can be loosened by hand.

Security

Where you park your bike, what you lock it with and what you lock it to are important in protecting it from being stolen.

- Buy the best lock you can afford.
- Lock your bike to something immovable in a well-lit public place.
- Locking two bikes together is better than locking them individually.
- Use a chain with a lock to secure the wheels and saddle to the frame. Keep a note of the frame number and other details, and insure, photograph and code the bike.

Canal towpaths

- In order to cycle along a canal towpath, you are required to have a permit from British Waterways. Local permits are free, but there is also – for a £5 fee – a national permit, which comes with information about all the towpaths under their care, and most useful of all, a key to facilities like showers and toilets. There are, however, some stretches of towpath you are not allowed to ride along on your bike. When you are cycling along a towpath, remember to give way to walkers and people using the canal. Call (01902) 409010, or write to: British Waterways, Willow Grange, Church Road, Watford WD1 3QA for further information.

Bicycles and trains

The combination of bicycle and train can make an excellent means of transport. In Great Britain, however, many new trains have been designed to hold the largest number of sitting passengers, and often have little or no space for bicycles.

But there are exceptions. The extensive network of local train services in the West Midlands County, sponsored by CENTRO (the West Midlands Passenger Transport Executive) and operated by Regional Railways Central, generally carries bicycles free and without restriction. Regional Railways Central has also adopted the same policy on these services when they run beyond the county boundary. The main services on which restrictions apply are between Coventry, Birmingham and Wolverhampton and between Wolverhampton and Shrewsbury.

Code of Conduct

- Enjoy the countryside and respect its life and work
- Only ride where you know you have a legal right
- Always yield to horses and pedestrians
- Take all litter with you
- Don't get annoyed with anyone; it never solves any problems
- Guard against all risk of fire
- Fasten all gates
- Keep your dogs under close control
- Keep to public paths across farmland
- Use gates and stiles to cross fences, hedges and walls
- Avoid livestock, crops and machinery or, if not possible, keep contact to a minimum
- Help keep all water clean
- Protect wildlife, plants and trees
- Take special care on country roads
- Make no unnecessary noise

Other operators also run services in the area covered by this book:

- **InterCity West Coast** and **InterCity Cross Country** trains call at Leamington Spa, Coventry, Birmingham, Wolverhampton, Nuneaton, Lichfield and Stafford. A few InterCity Cross Country trains cannot carry bicycles but usually they are carried for a fee. Reservations are required.

- **Regional Railways Central** cross country services run from Birmingham to Bromsgrove, Burton-on-Trent, Nuneaton and towards Shrewsbury carry bicycles for a fee. Reservations are required, there is limited space, and some trains do not take bicycles.

- **North London Railways** operate between Coventry and Birmingham, **Thames Trains** have services between Leamington Spa and Stratford and **Chiltern Trains** run between Birmingham and Leamington Spa. These operators do not accept bicycles during Monday-Friday peak hours, and there may be restrictions at other times.

> **!** *The above information has been checked and was believed to be correct at the time of writing. However, it may change during the lifetime of this book and you are strongly advised to check if any restrictions apply to your journey before setting out*

Rail information

ℂ Birmingham	0121 643 2711
ℂ Coventry	01203 555211
ℂ CENTRO, local rail information hotline	0121 200 2700
ℂ Severn Valley Railway	01299 403816

Legend to 1:50 000 maps

Roads and paths

Motorway

Service area   M 5   Elevated

Junction number **20**

Motorway under construction

Trunk road

Unfenced   Footbridge

A 46 (T)

Main road

Dual carriageway

A 420

Main road under construction

Secondary road

B 4348

Narrow road with passing places

A 855   B 885

Road generally more than 4 m wide

Bridge

Road generally less than 4 m wide

Other road, drive or track

Path

Gradient: 1 in 5 and steeper, 1 in 7 to 1 in 5

Gates   Road tunnel

Passenger ferry   Vehicle ferry

Ferry P   Ferry V

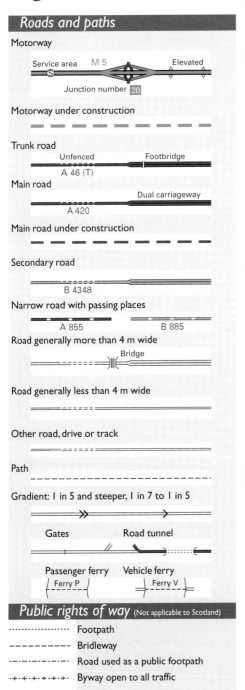

Public rights of way (Not applicable to Scotland)

····················	Footpath
– – – – – – – – –	Bridleway
·–·–·–·–·–·–	Road used as a public footpath
·+·+·+·+·+·+·	Byway open to all traffic

Danger Area   Firing and test ranges in the area. Danger! Observe warning notices

Tourist information

i	*i*	Information centre, all year / seasonal
P		Parking
✕		Picnic site
☆		Viewpoint
Å		Camp site
⚏		Caravan site
▲		Youth hostel
▨		Selected places of tourist interest
ℓ		Public telephone
ℓ		Motoring organisation telephone
⚑		Golf course or link
PC		Public convenience (in rural areas)

Railways

─────────	Track: multiple or single
·+·+·+·+·+·	Track: narrow gauge
)‖(	Bridges, footpath
⊞┅┅┅⊞	Tunnel
～～	Viaduct
┼─┼─┼	Freight line, siding or tramway
●─ a b ─⊞	Station, (a) principal, (b) closed to passengers
‖ LC	Level crossing
⊞⊞⊞⊞⊞	Embankment
⊞┅┅┅┅⊞	Cutting

Rock features

outcrop   cliff   650   600   scree

Water features

Canal (dry)
Canal
Aqueduct
Towpath
Lock
Ford
Normal tidal limit
Weir
Footbridge
Bridge
Lake
Slopes
Cliff
Flat rock
Sand
Dunes
Mud
High water mark
Low water mark
Lighthouse (in use)
Beacon
Lighthouse (disused)
Shingle

 Marsh or salting

General features

 Electricity transmission line (with pylons spaced conventionally)

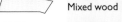 Pipeline (arrow indicates direction of flow)

 Buildings

Public buildings (selected)

🚌 Bus or coach station

Coniferous wood

Non-coniferous wood

Mixed wood

Orchard

Park or ornamental grounds

Quarry

Spoil heap, refuse tip or dump

Ŧ Radio or TV mast

i Church or chapel with tower

i Church or chapel with spire

+ Church or chapel without tower or spire

○ Chimney or tower

⌗ Glasshouse

+ Graticule intersection at 5' intervals

Ⓗ Heliport

△ Triangulation pillar

⥾ Windmill with or without sails

⥾ Windpump

Boundaries

+ — + — + National

—○—○—○—○—○— London borough

National park or forest park

NT National Trust

NT open access

NT limited access

—·—·—·—· County, region or islands area

+ · + · + · + District

Abbreviations

P   Post office
PH Public house
MS Milestone
MP Milepost
CH Clubhouse
PC Public convenience (in rural areas)
TH Town hall, guildhall or equivalent
CG Coastguard

Antiquities

VILLA Roman

Castle Non-Roman

⤬ Battlefield (with date)

✭ Tumulus

+ Position of antiquity which cannot be drawn to scale

ℳ Ancient monuments and historic buildings in the care of the Secretaries of State for the Environment, for Scotland and for Wales and that are open to the public

Heights

≈≈≈ 50 ≈≈≈ Contours are at 10 metres vertical interval

·144 Heights are to the nearest metre above mean sea level

Heights shown close to a triangulation pillar refer to the station height at ground level and not necessarily to the summit

From Lichfield along country lanes towards Cannock Chase through Fradley and Farewell

It comes as a surprise to find lanes so close to urban areas almost free of motor traffic. The Huddlesford to Alrewas leg is typical: quiet byways past woodlands and cornfields. Alrewas almost feels like a peaceful backwater with a proud high street and the core of the village hidden behind it. Close by is the once important junction of the Trent and Mersey with the Coventry canal, now often crowded with leisure craft. To Hanch the scenery is not so distinguished, the hangar of Fradley aerodrome being prominent. Then, suddenly, the monotony is replaced by variety with wood and hedgerows at Longdon giving way to ups and downs through Farewell.

Start

Lichfield City station

P As above

Distance and grade

20 miles

Easy/moderate

The route may also be combined with route 2. See route 2 for details

Terrain

An easy-going route, except for some short, sharp hills on the return leg from Longdon Green

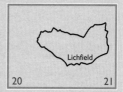
Nearest railway

Lichfield City
Lichfield Trent Valley CROSS CITY LINE: REDDITCH ▶ BIRMINGHAM ▶ LICHFIELD

Lichfield

20   21

Refreshments

Plenty of pubs in **Alrewas**
Swan PH, **Fradley Junction**
Red Lion PH, **Longdon Green**
Tea rooms and pubs in **Lichfield**

Lichfield

Alrewas

Whittington 2
Museum of the Staffordshire Regiment with a three-hundred year history showing uniforms, medals and weapons. St Giles' church has fine 15th-century stained glass windows. Of the original 13th-century building only the towers remain. The churchyard contains a memorial to Thomas Spencer (co-founder of the high street stores) who died in Whittington

Alrewas 5
Large village on the River Trent, historically associated with basket-weaving crafts, using wood from local alder and willow coppices, and with eel fishing

Fradley Junction 5/6
The vital link between the North of England, the Midlands and South-East in the pre-railway transport system. Characteristic canalside setting of pubs, cottages, boatyard, flight of narrow locks and a fine Wharf House, which actually pre-dates the canal

Hanch Hall 8
Mansion of 13th-century origin, now a mixture of Tudor, Jacobean, Queen Anne and Georgian architecture with a very fine Queen Anne facade

▼ *Fradley Junction on the Trent and Mersey canal*

1 R from Lichfield City station along main road (A5127) and R at X-roads (traffic lights) into Rotton Row. After 1 mile L at T-j onto Ryknild Street, then at roundabout R (3rd exit)

2 Under A38 road bridge and L, then L again at turn in Huddlesford immediately after crossing canal; SA at X-roads (NS), then L at T-j (NS)

3 After 1½ miles sharp L, then sharp R (NS). Opposite house sharp L, then SA across gated railway line; **take great care** and make sure gates are shut behind you

4 R at A38 T-j **take care** A38 is a very busy road. Use footpath on Derby bound side of A38 and after 150 yards take short path L to meet dead-end of Fox Lane.

5 L at offset X-roads onto A513 (**Or** SA, on Fox Lane, to visit Alrewas village). 1st L 'Fradley Village only'. SA at X-roads 'Lichfield'.

6 R at T-j 'Kings Bromley'

7 Turn L at A515 T-j (NS) and immediately after railway bridge R **easy to miss** then R at B5014 T-j (NS)

8 L at X-roads into Lysways Lane (NS). Follow to Longdon Green, passing under road bridge (A51). SA at X-roads 'Farewell, Chorley'

9 In Farewell L 'Lichfield'

10 At A51 T-j L (NS), R at traffic lights 'Streethay', then immediately R 'Lichfield Cathedral', SA at roundabout, continue SA, walking with bicycle up the Bird Street section. Keep SA to traffic lights at X-roads with A5127, where L for Lichfield City station

Link with route 2
See page 25 for details of how to combine routes 1 and 2

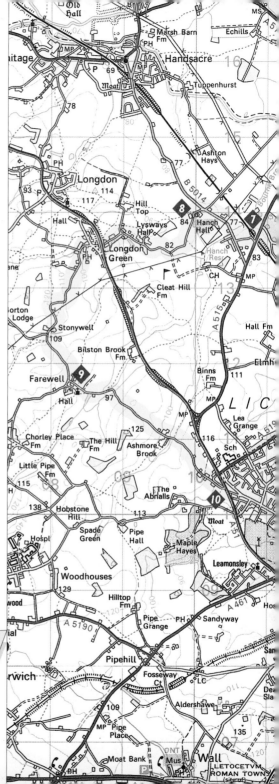

From Lichfield east through the villages of south Derbyshire and the Trent Valley

*T*his ride can be enjoyed on its own, as a medium length route over undulating country. It may, as well, be combined with route 1 to give a full day's ride for the less experienced cyclist. It runs through attractive villages with romantic-sounding names, the scenery changing from that of mixed farming in the south to lush meadows and pastures in the north. After the lovely stone bridge across the River Tame near Elford comes a series of quiet villages, some trim, some workaday; but the rural scene does not lack evidence of the nearby town and industry. North of Coton you are confronted by one of those paradoxes of the English countryside: patchwork pastureland with Friesians grazing, overshadowed by the great, stolid cooling towers of Burton's power station. The Vale of Trent was isolated in the past by dense forests and seasonal flooding; today the gravel pits are being converted into pools for angling and other water activities, and the power stations are nearing the end of their active lifespans.

Start

Lichfield City station
P As above

 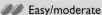
Distance and grade

25 miles
Easy/moderate

Terrain

From Lichfield downhill to the crossing of the Tame at Elford, followed by undulating country in Derbyshire. The Trent Valley is wide and open and the section in its flood plain is flat. Until the sudden rise before the final few miles back to Lichfield the hills are all in the distance

Nearest railway

Lichfield City
Lichfield Trent
Valley CROSS CITY LINE:
REDDITCH ▶ BIRMINGHAM ▶
LICHFIELD

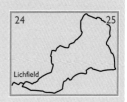

 Lichfield

Whittington

Harlaston

Haunton

Lullington

Lichfield 1

Compact and historic cathedral city with a country town atmosphere. In Bread Market Street is Dr Johnson's house and his statue stands next to the Heritage Centre housed in an old church with a viewing platform in the spire. A small cathedral, unique for the three spires (Ladies in the Vale) and the Minster and Stowe Pools. Two previous cathedrals stood on the site, pre-conquest Mercian then Norman but today's is largely 13th- and 14th-century

Elford 4

Off the beaten track but worth a short detour. Just south of the village a bronze age barrow (burial mound), reputedly used by Robin Hood as a shooting butt, survives today as a substantial circular mound

▲ Dr Samuel Johnson's birthplace, Lichfield

St Andrew's Church, Clifton Campville 6

St Andrew's Church, largely early 14th-century, has a notable buttressed steeple, reckoned one of the finest examples of medieval church architecture in Staffordshire

Rosliston Farm Forestry Centre 8

This new exhibition and demonstration centre explains the aims of the National Forest project

 Refreshments

Crown PH, **Elford**
White Lion PH, **Harlaston**
Green Man PH, **Clifton Campville**
Colville Arms PH, **Lullington**
Black Horse PH, **Coton in the Elms**
Plough PH, Bull's Head PH, **Rosliston**
White Swan PH, Shoulder of Mutton PH, **Walton-on-Trent**
Tea rooms and pubs in **Lichfield**

Rosliston

Walton-on-Trent

1 R from Lichfield City station along main road (A5127) and R at X-roads into Rotton Row

2 R at T-j after 1 mile onto Ryknild Street, then 2nd L Darnford Lane

3 At T-j bear L towards Whittington church (**not** sharp left 'Lichfield') and SA through Whittington village

4 After 2½ miles cross stone river bridge and R at A513 T-j 'Tamworth', then immediately L 'Harlaston' and L again at T-j 'Clifton Campville'

5 Bear R in Harlaston village. Continue SA through Haunton

6 In Clifton Campville L 'Lullington'. Climb hill into Derbyshire and continue SA through Lullington

7 ¾ mile after village R at T-j 'Coton' and in Coton R 'Rosliston', then fork L just before Black Horse PH 'Rosliston', L at T-j 'Walton, Burton', bear R in Rosliston 'Walton, Burton', then L 'Walton'

8 After 2 miles R at T-j 'Barton'

9 L at T-j 'Croxall'

10 After 3 miles R at A513 T-j 'Alrewas', then after ¾ mile L at X-roads (NS)

11 After ¾ mile bear R. Take next L, after ½ mile L again, then R after 150 yards

12 After 1¼ miles, where a belt of trees begins, fork R (NS), then SA at X-roads 'Lichfield'

13 R at X-roads in Huddlesford over canal and under railway, then R at T-j and under A38

14 L at roundabout Ryknild Street, then 2nd R Roman Way to return to Lichfield City railway station by reverse of outward route

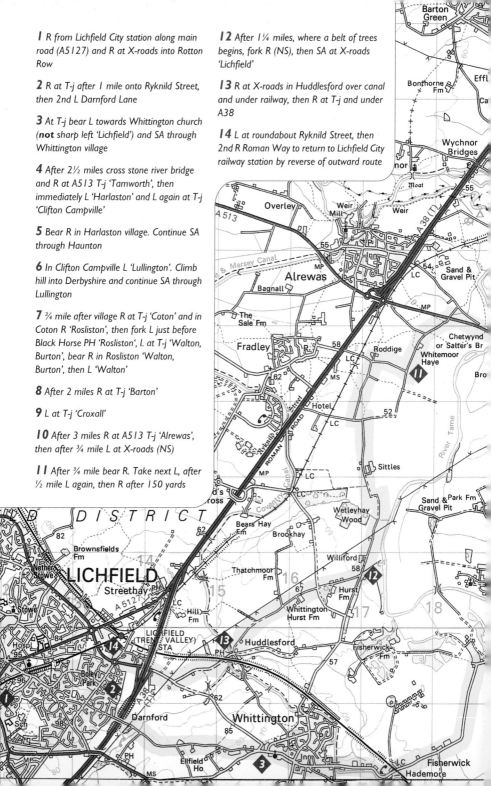

Link with route 1

This route may be combined with route 1 by following this route to instruction 10. Do not then turn L off A513 but, instead, SA along A513 over A38 arterial road, then 2nd R Fox Lane 'Alrewas' to pick up the instructions for route 1 at instruction 4 of that route, following them back to Lichfield (total distance 33 miles)

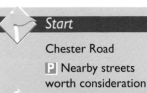

From Chester Road into easy countryside north-east of Birmingham visiting Kingsbury Water Park

 Start

Chester Road

P Nearby streets worth consideration

 Distance and grade

20 miles

Easy

 Terrain

A short beginner's ride over easy terrain and a suitable introductory route if you have older children with you. A summer evening's ride for the more energetic

Nearest railway

Chester Road

CROSS CITY LINE: REDDITCH ▶ BIRMINGHAM ▶ LICHFIELD

It is easy to get into the countryside from the north-east of Birmingham and within a couple of miles you will be on quiet lanes. To begin with these are straight and tree-lined but there is a sudden drop from Grove End into open mixed farming and woodland views. At Bodymoor Heath there is an interesting group of canalside buildings, including a Georgian inn. Beyond is the entrance to the Water Park. Across the park, reached with or without cycles – there are cycle racks in front of the park shop – is Kingsbury, marked by the handsome church tower overlooking the park. The return route passes through the rural hamlet of Lea Marston and modish Curdworth.

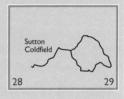

Sutton Coldfield

28   29

Chester Road station

Grove End

A 4097

Bodymoor Heath 6
On the Birmingham and Fazeley Canal with locks, canalside cottages and Georgian inn where canal boat horses were stabled overnight

Kingsbury Water Park 6
600 acres of lakes and picnic areas, nature reserves and footpaths. The pools were formed by floodwater off the Tame filling cavities left by gravel extraction. The visitor centre includes countryside shop, exhibition and café; admission is free with guided walks available

Kingsbury village
(off the route) 6/7
The Norman church (whose nave remains) was remodelled around 1300 with a quiet churchyard with yew trees, which is an attractive corner of this often functional village. Kingsbury Hall, separated from the church by a small ravine is a suitable disposition for a fortified medieval stone house

Curdworth 9
Church noted for its early wall paintings and Norman features including nave, chancel and font. The canal at this point is popular with anglers and has a short tunnel with a towpath

Refreshments

Dog and Doublet PH, **Bodymoor Heath**
Royal Oak PH, White Swan PH,
Kingsbury village
Swan PH, Railway PH, **Whitacre Heath**
Beehive PH, White Horse PH (at A4097 X-roads), village stores, **Curdworth**
Cock Inn PH, **Over Green**

Lea Marston

Curdworth

Grove End

1 L at Chester Road station onto Chester Road, L at traffic lights 'Sutton Coldfield A5127' and 4th R Penns Lane 'Walmley, Falcon Lodge' (just after pelican crossing)

2 L at X-roads into Walmley Road, then 1st R by memorial cross into Fox Hollies Road (NS). After ¾ mile L at roundabout into Thimble End Road. R at T-j and then L at next T-j

3 R at T-j 'Falcon Lodge', L at T-j 'Wishaw', then after ¾ mile R at T-j (NS)

4 After 1¼ miles bear L in Grove End, fork L (NS) just before A446 and L at T-j with A446 (NS), then after 130 yards R 'Hunts Green'

5 After ¾ mile R 'Bodymoor Heath' then R at T-j with A4091 and L 'Bodymoor Heath' and 'Kingsbury Water Park'. Cross canal, ignore L to Rare Breeds Farm, bear R over M42, then L 'Kingsbury Water Park'

6 On leaving park L, then SA at A4097 roundabout 'Whitacre Heath'

7 R in Whitacre Heath village 'Lea Marston'

8 L in Lea Marston 'Hams Hall, Lea Marston Church', then immediately R 'Hams Hall, Coleshill'. L at T-j with A446 'Coventry' then immediately R 'Curdworth' **take care**

9 At A4097 X-roads in Curdworth SA 'Wishaw' and over canal bridge. In Over Green village bear L (**not** sharp L) into Grove Lane

10 In Grove End village L into Oxleys Road and retrace original route (instruction 3 backwards) to Chester Road station

4 From Nuneaton to the birthplace of modern England

On this ride you will cycle through gently undulating mixed farming countryside, punctuated by church steeples which mark the mysteriously named Leicestershire villages. The scenery may not be spectacular but there is much in the scene to typify the English countryside: often pastoral, frequent stands of mature trees and a series of workman-like villages. There are commanding views from Higham and Orton. The tranquil lanes zigzag across the Ashby Canal. There is the chocolate box top appeal of Austrey, Market Bosworth and Stoke Golding, and the historical setting of Bosworth Field.

Start

Nuneaton station

P Long stay car park off Regent Street, close to Nuneaton station

Distance and grade

30 miles (may be shortened by using the steam railway for part of the trip)

Easy/moderate

Terrain

The land on the Leicestershire / Warwickshire border is gently undulating but there are one or two hills to climb – as village names testify. It is ideal for the less energetic, or if you have children with you. Be wary on the blind hump-back canal bridges

Nearest railway

Nuneaton REGIONAL RAILWAYS: BIRMINGHAM ► COVENTRY ► LEICESTER INTERCITY WEST COAST MAIN LINE

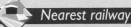

Nuneaton | Higham on the Hill | Upton | Sibson | Sheepy Parva | Orton-on-the-Hill | Austrey | Appleby M

Sheepy Magna 5
The River Sence, with prominent water mill and gossamer millpool, divides Parva and Magna. All Saints' has two windows by William Morris, one by Burne Jones and one by Kemp, reckoned second only to Morris as a late Victorian artist in stained glass

Refreshments

Cock Inn, **Sibson**
Black Horse PH, **Sheepy Magna**
Picnic place by River Sence (Post Office & Stores sells sandwiches), Bird in Hand PH, **Austrey**
Belper Arms PH, **Newton Burgoland**
The Victorian Tea Room,
Shackerstone Station
Plenty of tea shops and pubs
in **Market Bosworth**
Battlefield Centre café, **Shenton**

Twycross Zoo (near Norton- Juxta-Twycross) 6/7
Includes a reptile house, butterfly and insect houses

The Battlefield Line
Between 8 and 11
The Ashby to Nuneaton rail line has, in part, been re-opened by enthusiasts (Shackerstone to Shenton). Shackerstone station is now a treasury of railway relics with an excellent tea room; there are regular steam and diesel services to the battlefield in summer

Market Bosworth 10
Engaging market place which is a legacy of the town's medieval importance. Nearby is a grammar school founded by Sir Wolstan Dixie where Dr Samuel Johnson once taught. The present building is Tudor style but was built in 1828. Many memorials to other members of the Dixie family can be found in the 14th- and 15th-century church. The hall was built in the early 1700's in the style of Hampton Court

Bosworth Field 10/11
The bloody battle of Bosworth Field (1485) put an end to feudal England. King Richard III was slain and Henry Tudor went on to begin the creation of a centralised state. The battle over Richard's reputation (monster or martyr?) continues. The landscape, now marked out with the positions of the battle, creates a powerful and haunting memorial. The Battlefield Centre has exhibitions, films, books and a café

Snarestone   Newton Burgoland   Congerstone   Market Bosworth   Stoke Golding   Higham-on-the-Hill

1 L at exit from Nuneaton station and immediately L Regent Street L at T-j, then R 'A47 Hinckley'. At mini-roundabout L 'Higham', then at A5 roundabout **take care**, and SA up to Higham

2 R at T-j 'Stoke Golding, Market Bosworth'. Fork L at end of village 'Stoke Gregory'

3 After 1 mile L at X-roads 'Upton, Sibson'. L at T-j 'Upton, Sibson'. L at T-j 'Upton, Fenny Drayton' and immediately R 'Upton' to village. 1 mile after Upton L at T-j 'Sibson'

4 R for 300 yards at T-j with A444, then 1st L (Cock Inn) 'Sheepy Magna' through Sibson

5 In Sheepy Parva R at T-j with B585 'Wellsborough' and on bend L onto minor lane 'unsuitable for motors', through ford. L onto road. SA at X-roads with B4116 'Orton on the Hill'

➡ **page 35**

11 After village green R 'Stoke Golding'. R at T-j in Stoke 'Higham'. 1st L 'Higham'.

12 Cross R over canal, then SA at X-roads and then return via Higham to Nuneaton by retracing outward route from instruction 2 backwards

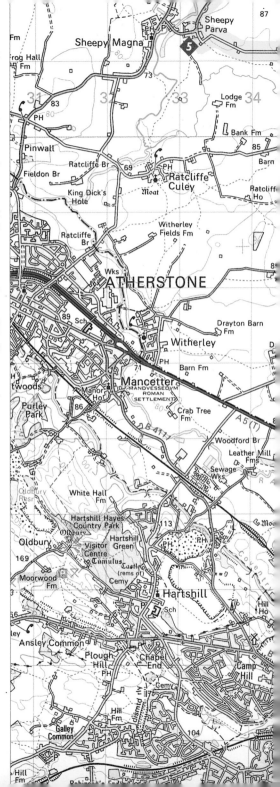

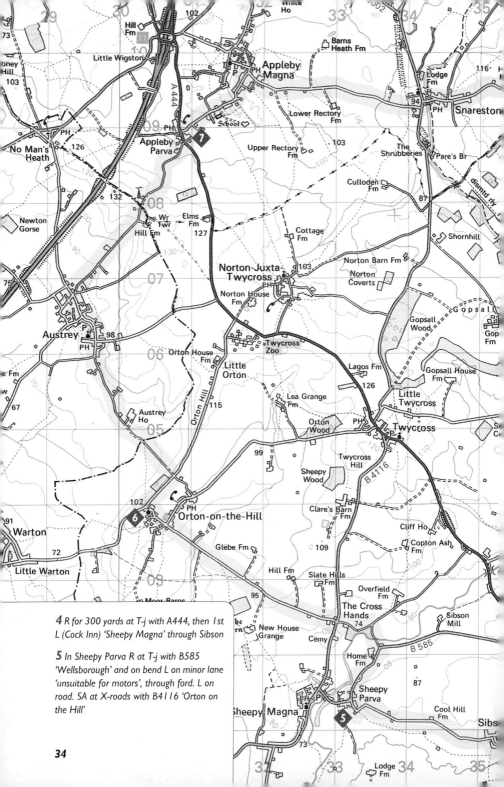

4 R for 300 yards at T-j with A444, then 1st L (Cock Inn) 'Sheepy Magna' through Sibson

5 In Sheepy Parva R at T-j with B585 'Wellsborough' and on bend L on minor lane 'unsuitable for motors', through ford. L on road. SA at X-roads with B4116 'Orton on the Hill'

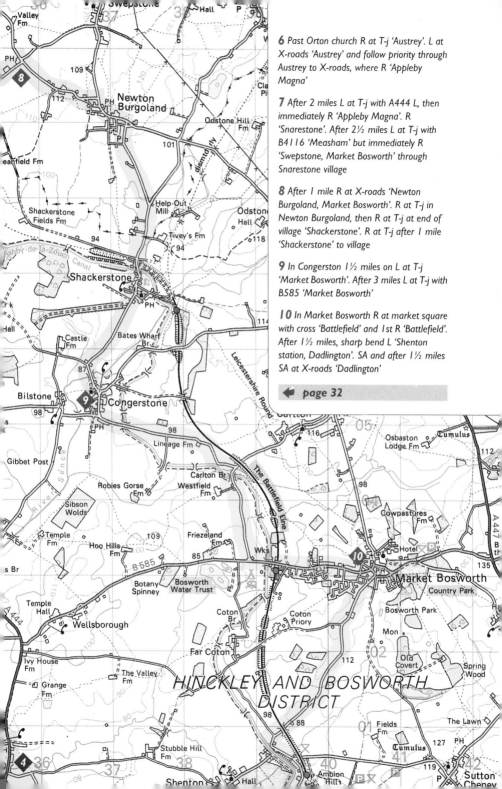

6 Past Orton church R at T-j 'Austrey'. L at X-roads 'Austrey' and follow priority through Austrey to X-roads, where R 'Appleby Magna'

7 After 2 miles L at T-j with A444 L, then immediately R 'Appleby Magna'. R 'Snarestone'. After 2½ miles L at T-j with B4116 'Measham' but immediately R 'Swepstone, Market Bosworth' through Snarestone village

8 After 1 mile R at X-roads 'Newton Burgoland, Market Bosworth'. R at T-j in Newton Burgoland, then R at T-j at end of village 'Shackerstone'. R at T-j after 1 mile 'Shackerstone' to village

9 In Congerston 1½ miles on L at T-j 'Market Bosworth'. After 3 miles L at T-j with B585 'Market Bosworth'

10 In Market Bosworth R at market square with cross 'Battlefield' and 1st R 'Battlefield'. After 1½ miles, sharp bend L 'Shenton station, Dadlington'. SA and after 1½ miles SA at X-roads 'Dadlington'

← page 32

5 From Coventry visiting the diverse villages of the green belt between Birmingham and Coventry

A fairly strenuous ride with some pronounced climbs, especially before Meriden. One of the toughest, out of Fillongley, can be avoided with a short cut but there are excellent views on the long route before descending into Maxstoke. The route crosses some of the upland countryside of north Warwickshire and offers a series of sweeping views, both pastoral and urban. The sequence of villages visited takes in Fillongley in the former mining district; Meriden, the shrine of many keen cyclists; picturesque Berkswell; and Balsall Common, a piece of redbrick suburbia puzzlingly severed from Solihull. The highlight of the ride is a delightful 'lost' lane soon after the bustle of Balsall Common, culminating in a rise up to Temple Balsall.

Start

Coventry station

P Grosvenor Road (leave station to large roundabout SA 'Birmingham A45' then 1st L) and in Queen Victoria Road. High charges during the week but may be cheaper at weekends

Distance and grade

36 miles (full route) or 32 miles (short cut)
Moderate

Terrain

A route with a number of hills. North of the arterial road between Coventry and Birmingham the ground rises, and there is a climb from Coventry up to Fillongley. The short route cuts out the steepest part. Beyond Meriden the land is more undulating

Coventry

Brownshill Green

Corley Moor

Fillongley

Maxstoke

Nearest railway

🚉 Coventry 🚏 *INTERCITY*
WEST COAST MAIN LINE
🚏 *REGIONAL RAILWAYS CENTRAL*

🚉 Berkswell
🚉 Tile Hill
🚏 *BIRMINGHAM ▶ COVENTRY*

Refreshments

Bull and Butcher PH, Red Lion PH, **Corley Moor**
Manor House PH, Butchers Arms PH, **Fillongley**
Cottage Inn, just outside **Fillongley**
Newsagent, shop, **Meriden**
Bear Inn PH, cream teas some Sunday
afternoons in Village Hall, **Berkswell**
Teas at The Old School Room,
Temple Balsall   *Tipperary Inn,* **Meer End**

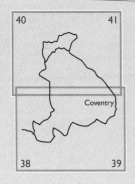

Places of interest

Maxstoke Priory and Castle 6/7

The ruins of an Augustinian priory founded in 1339 by William de Clinton. Two sides of a central tower and an outer gatehouse are visible from the road. To reach the castle go through Maxstoke, then L at T-j and 1st R into Castle Road

Meriden 7

The geographical centre of England. The small green retains its ancient cross and has a memorial to the cyclists killed in the World Wars

Berkswell 7/8

Beautiful, individualistic village with very friendly inhabitants. The church, probably the finest Norman church in the county, dates from 1150, but its most striking feature is the 16th-century two-storey timber porch. A museum of rural bygones in a 16th-century cottage behind the almshouses is worth visiting

Temple Balsall 10

A satisfying collection of buildings, consisting of a Templars' chapel (now the parish church), 17th-century almshouses and Temple Hall. The village began as a centre for the Knights Templars and, after their suppression, by the Knights Hospitallers, in turn ejected at the Dissolution in 1538–40

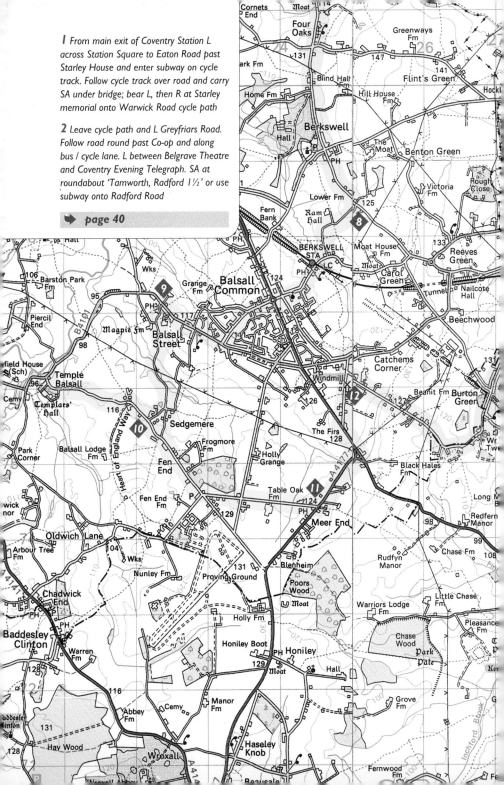

1 From main exit of Coventry Station L across Station Square to Eaton Road past Starley House and enter subway on cycle track. Follow cycle track over road and carry SA under bridge; bear L, then R at Starley memorial onto Warwick Road cycle path

2 Leave cycle path and L Greyfriars Road. Follow road round past Co-op and along bus / cycle lane. L between Belgrave Theatre and Coventry Evening Telegraph. SA at roundabout 'Tamworth, Radford 1½' or use subway onto Radford Road

➡ *page 40*

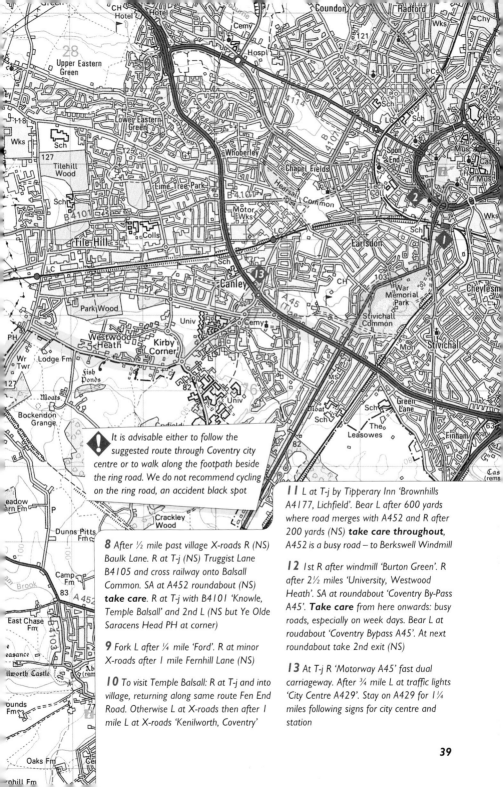

It is advisable either to follow the suggested route through Coventry city centre or to walk along the footpath beside the ring road. We do not recommend cycling on the ring road, an accident black spot

8 After ½ mile past village X-roads R (NS) Baulk Lane. R at T-j (NS) Truggist Lane B4105 and cross railway onto Balsall Common. SA at A452 roundabout (NS) **take care**. R at T-j with B4101 'Knowle, Temple Balsall' and 2nd L (NS but Ye Olde Saracens Head PH at corner)

9 Fork L after ¼ mile 'Ford'. R at minor X-roads after 1 mile Fernhill Lane (NS)

10 To visit Temple Balsall: R at T-j and into village, returning along same route Fen End Road. Otherwise L at X-roads then after 1 mile L at X-roads 'Kenilworth, Coventry'

11 L at T-j by Tipperary Inn 'Brownhills A4177, Lichfield'. Bear L after 600 yards where road merges with A452 and R after 200 yards (NS) **take care throughout**, A452 is a busy road – to Berkswell Windmill

12 1st R after windmill 'Burton Green'. R after 2½ miles 'University, Westwood Heath'. SA at roundabout 'Coventry By-Pass A45'. **Take care** from here onwards: busy roads, especially on week days. Bear L at roudabout 'Coventry Bypass A45'. At next roundabout take 2nd exit (NS)

13 At T-j R 'Motorway A45' fast dual carriageway. After ¾ mile L at traffic lights 'City Centre A429'. Stay on A429 for 1¼ miles following signs for city centre and station

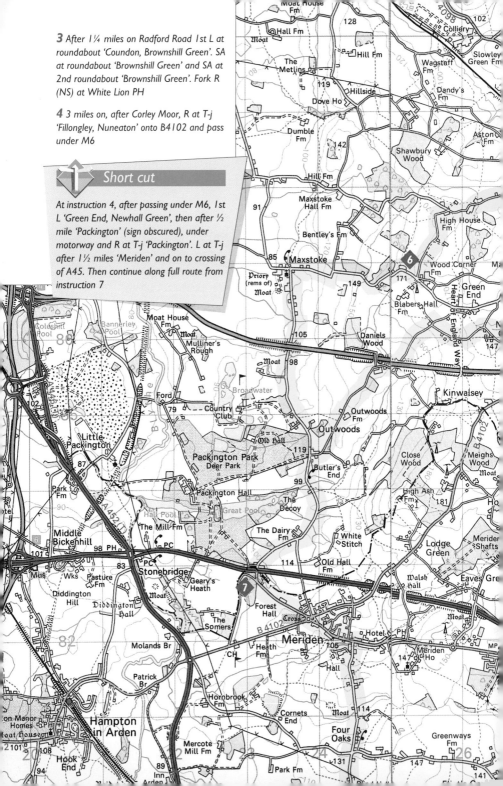

3 After 1¼ miles on Radford Road 1st L at roundabout 'Coundon, Brownshill Green'. SA at roundabout 'Brownshill Green' and SA at 2nd roundabout 'Brownshill Green'. Fork R (NS) at White Lion PH

4 3 miles on, after Corley Moor, R at T-j 'Fillongley, Nuneaton' onto B4102 and pass under M6

Short cut

At instruction 4, after passing under M6, 1st L 'Green End, Newhall Green', then after ½ mile 'Packington' (sign obscured), under motorway and R at T-j 'Packington'. L at T-j after 1½ miles 'Meriden' and on to crossing of A45. Then continue along full route from instruction 7

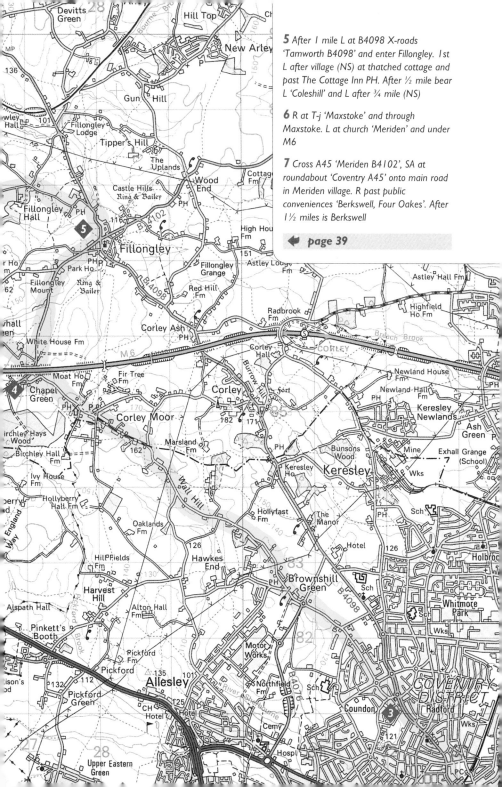

5 After 1 mile L at B4098 X-roads 'Tamworth B4098' and enter Fillongley. 1st L after village (NS) at thatched cottage and past The Cottage Inn PH. After ½ mile bear L 'Coleshill' and L after ¾ mile (NS)

6 R at T-j 'Maxstoke' and through Maxstoke. L at church 'Meriden' and under M6

7 Cross A45 'Meriden B4102', SA at roundabout 'Coventry A45' onto main road in Meriden village. R past public conveniences 'Berkswell, Four Oakes'. After 1 ½ miles is Berkswell

◀ **page 39**

6 From Dorridge past medieval houses and through relics of the Forest of Arden to a romantic ruined castle

Start

Dorridge station

P Long stay car park in Grange Road (R before railway bridge as approaching Dorridge centre from south)

Distance and grade

31 miles

Easy

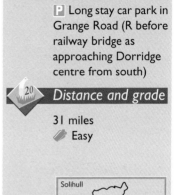

An easy ride without any steep hills, passing through the gently undulating country ideal for cycling to the south-east of Solihull. In medieval times the area was in the Forest of Arden and for the first section of the route, to Beausale, there is still an abundance of trees. From Beausale to Kenilworth is a complete contrast. It is more like the Feldon region, south of Warwick, with its large open views. This is the eastern edge of the Birmingham Plateau and the land drops away to the lower

Refreshments

Teashop, restaurant, **Dorridge**
Railway PH, on ride ½ mile outside **Dorridge**
Restaurant at **Baddesley Clinton**
Case is Altered PH, **Five Ways**
Plenty of teashops and pubs in **Kenilworth**
Railway PH, **Balsall Common** (off route in Baulk Lane)
Bear Inn, **Berkswell**

ground of the East Midlands. On the return from Kenilworth the scenery is a mixture of the first two sections. The ride also becomes distinctly sociable, at least on a Sunday, with a visit to Mrs Field's Berkswell Windmill and the chance of tea with the ladies of the Women's Institute in Berkswell village.

Dorridge station

Baddesley Clinton

Beausale

Park Pale

Terrain

Lanes and close views near Dorridge, once in the Forest of Arden, contrast with the open landscape near Kenilworth, resembling south-east Warwickshire. Both parts are, however, gently undulating – ideal cycling country

Nearest railway

🚂 Dorridge
🚉 *LEAMINGTON SPA* ►
BIRMINGHAM

🚂 Berkswell
🚉 *BIRMINGHAM* ► *COVENTRY*

▼ *Kenilworth Castle*

Places of interest

Packwood House 2
A Tudor house with distinctive yew garden depicting the Sermon on the Mount and sundials on several walls

Baddesley Clinton Hall and Church 3
The Hall, also owned by the National Trust, is an outstanding medieval moated manor house built in grey stone and set in 120 acres of parkland; it dates from the 13th century. The church at the end of a tree-lined footpath is well worth a visit.

Hay Wood 3/4
Approximately 1 mile down Haywood Lane on L. No signposts to entrance to wood or for pleasant woodland walks but inside there are picnic tables at the entrance among the trees

Kenilworth Castle 7
Once a stronghold of King John in the 13th century, the castle was given by Queen Elizabeth of England to her favourite, Robert Dudley, Earl of Leicester. The ruins are open to the public and merit a visit

43

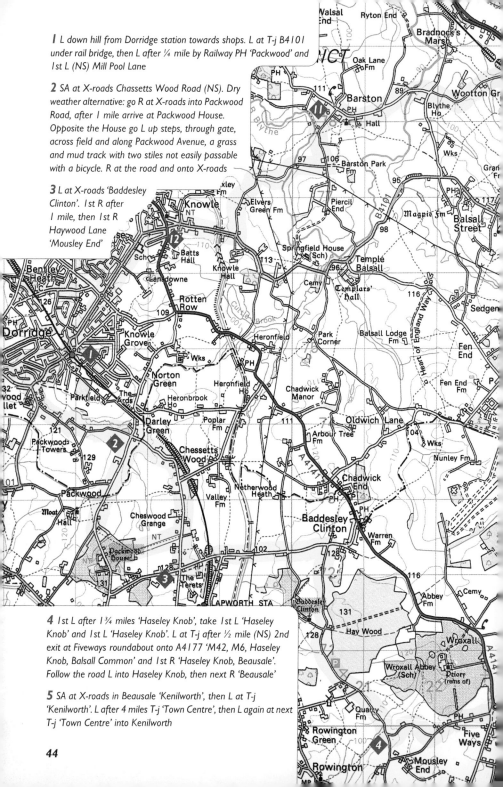

1 L down hill from Dorridge station towards shops. L at T-j B4101 under rail bridge, then L after ¼ mile by Railway PH 'Packwood' and 1st L (NS) Mill Pool Lane

2 SA at X-roads Chassetts Wood Road (NS). Dry weather alternative: go R at X-roads into Packwood Road, after 1 mile arrive at Packwood House. Opposite the House go L up steps, through gate, across field and along Packwood Avenue, a grass and mud track with two stiles not easily passable with a bicycle. R at the road and onto X-roads

3 L at X-roads 'Baddesley Clinton'. 1st R after 1 mile, then 1st R Haywood Lane 'Mousley End'

4 1st L after 1¾ miles 'Haseley Knob', take 1st L 'Haseley Knob' and 1st L 'Haseley Knob'. L at T-j after ½ mile (NS) 2nd exit at Fiveways roundabout onto A4177 'M42, M6, Haseley Knob, Balsall Common' and 1st R 'Haseley Knob, Beausale'. Follow the road L into Haseley Knob, then next R 'Beausale'

5 SA at X-roads in Beausale 'Kenilworth', then L at T-j 'Kenilworth'. L after 4 miles T-j 'Town Centre', then L again at next T-j 'Town Centre' into Kenilworth

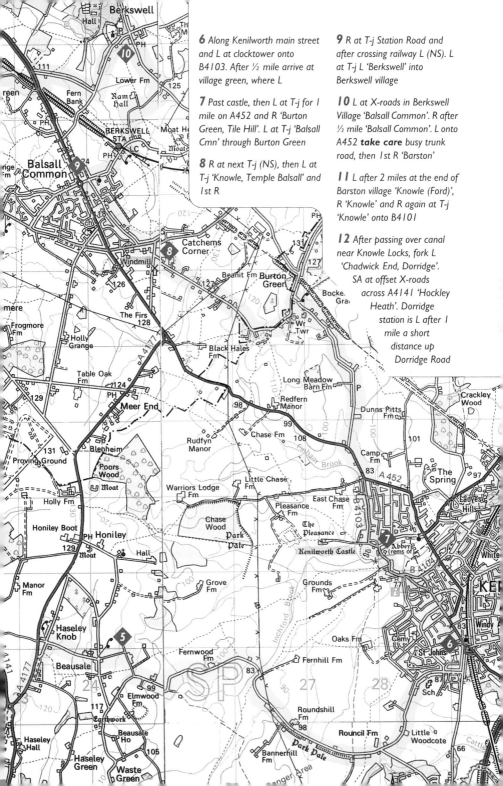

6 Along Kenilworth main street and L at clocktower onto B4103. After ½ mile arrive at village green, where L

7 Past castle, then L at T-j for 1 mile on A452 and R 'Burton Green, Tile Hill'. L at T-j 'Balsall Cmn' through Burton Green

8 R at next T-j (NS), then L at T-j 'Knowle, Temple Balsall' and 1st R

9 R at T-j Station Road and after crossing railway L (NS). L at T-j L 'Berkswell' into Berkswell village

10 L at X-roads in Berkswell Village 'Balsall Common'. R after ½ mile 'Balsall Common'. L onto A452 **take care** busy trunk road, then 1st R 'Barston'

11 L after 2 miles at the end of Barston village 'Knowle (Ford)', R 'Knowle' and R again at T-j 'Knowle' onto B4101

12 After passing over canal near Knowle Locks, fork L 'Chadwick End, Dorridge'. SA at offset X-roads across A4141 'Hockley Heath'. Dorridge station is L after 1 mile a short distance up Dorridge Road

From Leamington to Charlecote Park and the historic town of Warwick

Start

Leamington Spa station

P As above

Distance and grade

47 miles

Easy/moderate

Terrain

The Feldon is an undulating landscape with few steep hills. Strong winds may be a problem because of the relative flatness and lack of cover

The Warwickshire Feldon, or field area, is the undulating land between the Avon and the Cotswolds. The landscape with large open cornfields and few trees is very different from the wooded pastures of the Forest of Arden north of the river. The Feldon has been cultivated extensively since the New Stone Age and many fields still show the ridge and furrow produced by medieval ploughing. The route is shown by name on the OS Landranger Sheet 151 Stratford-upon-Avon.

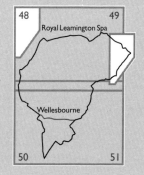

Refreshments

Fox and Hen PH, **Bascote Heath**
Plenty of pubs and shops in **Harbury**
Antelope PH, stores, **Lighthorne**
Teas and light meals, The Orangery, **Charlecote Park**
Plenty of teashops and pubs in **Warwick**
Café in Jephson Park, **Leamington**

Royal Leamington Spa

Offchurch

Bascote Heath

Harbury

Lighthorne

🚃 Leamington Spa
🚃 Warwick
🚲 *BIRMINGHAM ▶ STRATFORD-UPON-AVON ▶ LEAMINGTON SPA*

Places of interest

Royal Leamington Spa 1
A fine Regency spa town laid out around gardens and river. A railway line marks the southern edge of the town centre. For gardens and Tourist Information Office in Jephson Gardens, L from station, L at traffic lights beyond railway bridge and on R along the Parade

Chesterton Windmill 7
Built in stone it is very unusual and striking and was erected in 1632 to a neo-classical design by Inigo Jones. Enter by the gate at the turn at top of the hill, notice the water mill below

Charlecote Park and House 14
Beautiful house owned by the National Trust. A young Shakespeare is claimed to have poached deer here. The restored working watermill of about 1800, can be approached by footpath from the bridge just before Hampton Lucy. Telephone Charlecote Mill beforehand if you wish to visit

Warwick 17
The castle requires a whole day to explore. St Mary's Church (L from High Street) has an impressive chapel, tombs of the Earls of Warwick and an atmospheric Norman crypt. Lord Leycester's hospital, just after gate arch, is most definitely worth a visit, as is the Doll Museum in Castle Street and Mill Garden in Mill Street (above the bridge)

▲ *Warwick Castle*

Combrook

Walton

Wellesbourne

Hampton Lucy

Warwick

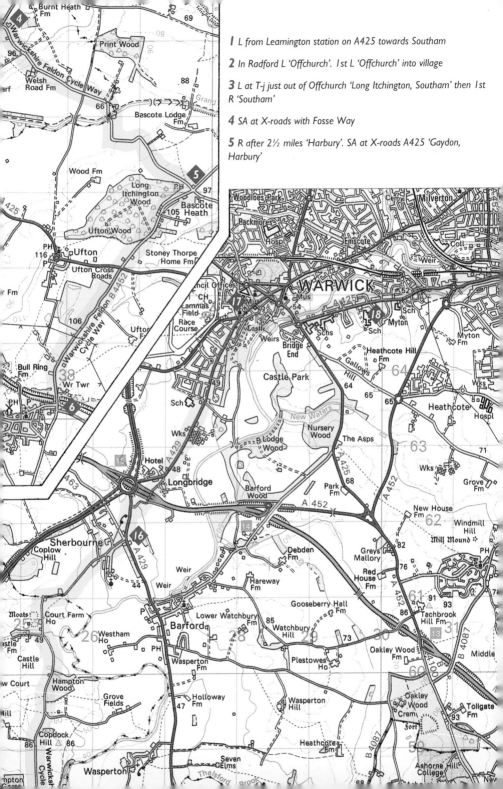

1 L from Leamington station on A425 towards Southam

2 In Radford L 'Offchurch'. 1st L 'Offchurch' into village

3 L at T-j just out of Offchurch 'Long Itchington, Southam' then 1st R 'Southam'

4 SA at X-roads with Fosse Way

5 R after 2½ miles 'Harbury'. SA at X-roads A425 'Gaydon, Harbury'

6 R after 1 ½ miles 'Harbury'. In Harbury R 'Village Centre'. SA at X-roads in High Street, then 1st L Chapel Lane. R at T-j 'Chesterton'

7 After 1 ½ miles L at windmill 'Chesterton, Ashorne'. 1st L 'Chesterton'. R in village

➡ **page 51**

16 R at T-j in Sherbourne, immediately L A429 and after 200 yards R on cycletrack 'Warwick' and over motorway

17 In Warwick SA at church over gateway into High Street. R at East Gate traffic lights and down Castle Hill 'Southam, Banbury'. Across bridge and L A425 'Southam, Leamington'

18 R after ½ mile Queensway Cycle Track via Samur Lane. Follow path across canal to pedestrian traffic lights, dismount to cross then R A425 to Leamington station

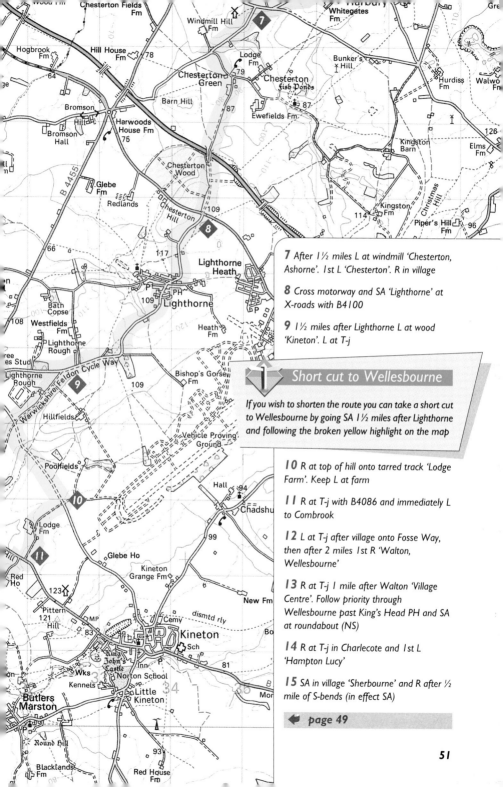

7 After 1½ miles L at windmill 'Chesterton, Ashorne'. 1st L 'Chesterton'. R in village

8 Cross motorway and SA 'Lighthorne' at X-roads with B4100

9 1½ miles after Lighthorne L at wood 'Kineton'. L at T-j

⟨1⟩ Short cut to Wellesbourne

If you wish to shorten the route you can take a short cut to Wellesbourne by going SA 1½ miles after Lighthorne and following the broken yellow highlight on the map

10 R at top of hill onto tarred track 'Lodge Farm'. Keep L at farm

11 R at T-j with B4086 and immediately L to Combrook

12 L at T-j after village onto Fosse Way, then after 2 miles 1st R 'Walton, Wellesbourne'

13 R at T-j 1 mile after Walton 'Village Centre'. Follow priority through Wellesbourne past King's Head PH and SA at roundabout (NS)

14 R at T-j in Charlecote and 1st L 'Hampton Lucy'

15 SA in village 'Sherbourne' and R after ½ mile of S-bends (in effect SA)

← page 49

From Dorridge to Stratford-upon-Avon returning via Wilmcote

A fair day's ride but without any lengthy hills to climb, through what was once the Forest of Arden to the inevitable honeypot destination of the Midlands. Many older Brummies have fond memories of days out by bicycle to Stratford. The ride down to Stratford affords splendid panoramas of the Avon Valley with the Feldon and Cotswolds beyond; none better than that from the war memorial cross at Snitterfield. The return route threads its way along a skein of often narrow, quiet country lanes, which feels more uphill than the outward journey.

Start

Dorridge station

P Long stay car park in Grange Road (on far side of railway line from station entrance)

Distance and grade

43 miles (37 miles if going from Snitterfield to instruction 9 by way of Bearley)

Easy/moderate

Terrain

The going is generally easy, through what was once the Forest of Arden, with some climbs which can be taken gently

▶ Mary Arden's cottage, Wilmcote

Refreshments

Fleur de Lys PH, **Lowsonford**
Red Lion PH, **Claverdon**
Foxhunter PH, Snitterfield Arms PH, **Snitterfield**
Plenty of pubs and cafés in **Stratford**
Teas at Mary Arden's House, **Wilmcote**
King's Head PH, **Aston Cantlow**

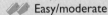

Dorridge station   Lowsonford   Holywell   Wolverton   Snitterfield   Welcombe Hills Country Park   Stratford-upon-A

Nearest railway

🚉 Dorridge ⊖ BIRMING-
HAM ▶ LEAMINGTON SPA

🚉 Wood End
🚉 Wilmcote
🚉 Stratford-upon-
Avon ⊖ BIRMINGHAM ▶
STRATFORD-UPON-AVON

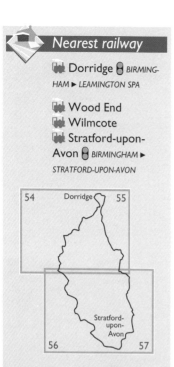

Places of interest

Stratford-upon-Avon 7

For cyclists, this is the home of Pashley cycles (L at lights at the end of Clopton Road, shop is then on R) and Shakespeare. A fording place across the river Avon since Celtic times, the first recorded settlement was in 691 AD, when there was a monastery on the site of the present parish church. The Bishop of Worcester established a market town in the 12th century. Shakespearean properties, the local history museum (Nash's House, Chapel Street) and the brass rubbing centre (Avonbank Gardens, near the theatre) are worth visiting

Stratford-upon-Avon Canal 3/4 and 7

The canal was opened in 1816 and meant to link the industrial Black Country with the Severn via Stratford and the Warwickshire Avon. The iron aqueduct at Bearley is the longest one in England, with the 200-yard-long trough being carried on 13 brick piers

Wilmcote • Shelfield • Oldberrow • Ullenhall • Danzey Green • Nuthurst • Packwood

53

1 L out of Dorridge station down hill towards shops. L at T-j Grange Lane under rail bridge and L by railway PH L 'Packwood'

2 L at T-j (NS) and immediately R at further T-j 'Lapworth 2, Packwood House'. Pass through grounds of Packwood House and R at T-j (in effect SA) 'Lapworth 1, Hockley Heath 2, Warwick 8', then 1st L on RH bend (in effect SA) 'Lapworth, Warwick B4439'

3 L at T-j 'Lapworth ½, Warwick 8 B4439' over canal bridge, 1st R Lapworth Street 'Lowsonford 2¼' and over M40 after 1¼ miles

4 In Lowsonford go past 'Fleur-de-Lys' PH, then L 'Shrewley 1½, Warwick 6' at village hall and over canal bridge. R 'High Cross ¼' by black and white timbered building, then on LH bend R 'Holywell ½' downhill into narrow road **easy to miss** large tree near the junction, signpost arm for this direction not easily visible from main road and R at T-j 'Claverdon ¼'

5 L at T-j in village (opposite shop) Station Road 'Warwick 6 A4189'. After 1 mile pass over railway, then 1st R 'Wolverton 1½, Snitterfield 3'

➡ **page 56**

11 After 1 mile R 'Oldberrow, Henley 2'. At T-j by Church L 'Redditch A4189, Ullenhall 1' **take care** fast moving traffic and 1st R (after Cadborough Farm) 'Ullenhall ½'

12 L at T-j in Ullenhall village then immediately R into Watery Lane. At T-j R 'Danzey Green 1', then L at next T-j at the east end of Gentlemans Lane and after passing under railway bridge L at T-j 'Tanworth 1¼'

13 1st R 'Earlswood 3' (before bridge over railway), then R at T-j 'Henley 3½', 1st L 'Hockley Heath 1, Lapworth 2½' and 1st R **easy to miss** (NS)

14 At busy A3400 T-j **take care** L, then immediately R into Wharf Lane (NS) and R at T-j with B4439, then immediately L into 'Packwood 1¼'. R at T-j after passing church drive (NS)

15 L at T-j into Packwood Road 'Knowle 3, Solihull 6' (early in the ride the route went R at this T-j), pass under railway bridge, then L into Blue Lake Road (NS) and 1st L into Dorridge Road (NS) back to Dorridge Station

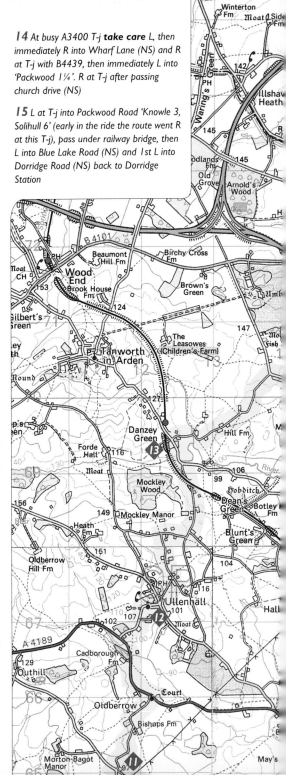

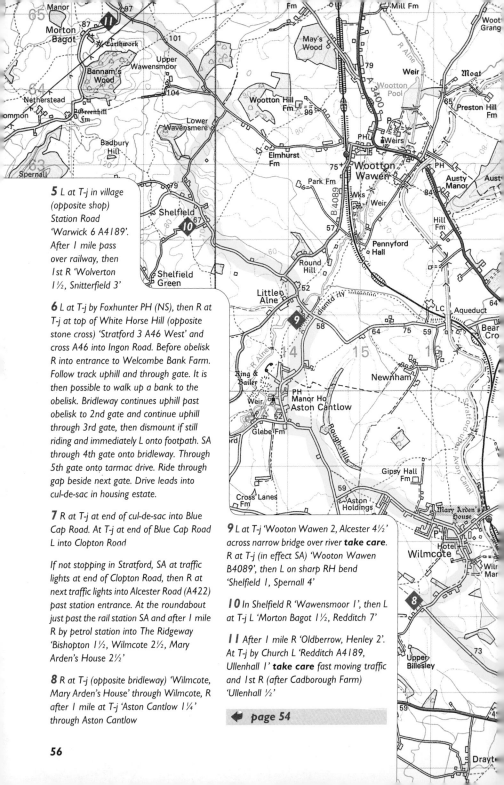

5 L at T-j in village (opposite shop) Station Road 'Warwick 6 A4189'. After 1 mile pass over railway, then 1st R 'Wolverton 1½, Snitterfield 3'

6 L at T-j by Foxhunter PH (NS), then R at T-j at top of White Horse Hill (opposite stone cross) 'Stratford 3 A46 West' and cross A46 into Ingon Road. Before obelisk R into entrance to Welcombe Bank Farm. Follow track uphill and through gate. It is then possible to walk up a bank to the obelisk. Bridleway continues uphill past obelisk to 2nd gate and continue uphill through 3rd gate, then dismount if still riding and immediately L onto footpath. SA through 4th gate onto bridleway. Through 5th gate onto tarmac drive. Ride through gap beside next gate. Drive leads into cul-de-sac in housing estate.

7 R at T-j at end of cul-de-sac into Blue Cap Road. At T-j at end of Blue Cap Road L into Clopton Road

If not stopping in Stratford, SA at traffic lights at end of Clopton Road, then R at next traffic lights into Alcester Road (A422) past station entrance. At the roundabout just past the rail station SA and after 1 mile R by petrol station into The Ridgeway 'Bishopton 1½, Wilmcote 2½, Mary Arden's House 2½'

8 R at T-j (opposite bridleway) 'Wilmcote, Mary Arden's House' through Wilmcote, R after 1 mile at T-j 'Aston Cantlow 1¼' through Aston Cantlow

9 L at T-j 'Wooton Wawen 2, Alcester 4½' across narrow bridge over river **take care**. R at T-j (in effect SA) 'Wooton Wawen B4089', then L on sharp RH bend 'Shelfield 1, Spernall 4'

10 In Shelfield R 'Wawensmoor 1', then L at T-j L 'Morton Bagot 1½, Redditch 7'

11 After 1 mile R 'Oldborrow, Henley 2'. At T-j by Church L 'Redditch A4189, Ullenhall 1' **take care** fast moving traffic and 1st R (after Cadborough Farm) 'Ullenhall ½'

◀ **page 54**

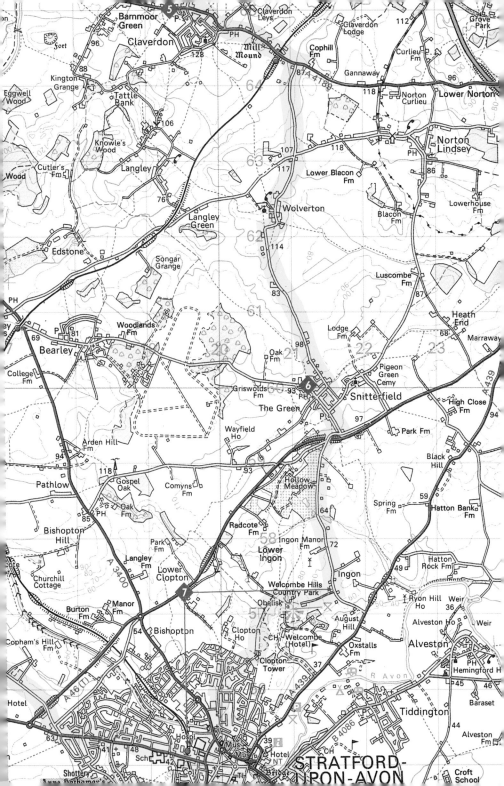

9 From Yardley Wood station to the village of Tanworth, returning by ancient sunken lanes

Start

Yardley Wood station

P As above

Distance and grade

22 miles

Easy/moderate

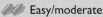

Terrain

An ideal route for people new to leisure cycle touring. There are one or two short climbs. The quiet middle of the route, between Gorcott Hill and Forhill, is generally on poorly surfaced minor roads and tracks and has steepish uphill sections

This short ride through country in the medieval Forest of Arden is an ideal beginners' route over easy terrain. Once out of the city, the route follows quiet Warwickshire lanes to the picture-postcard village of Tanworth-in-Arden (the suffix is to distinguish it from the town of Tamworth to the north-east of Birmingham). The second half of the route is in Worcestershire and takes in perhaps the best section of Roman road in the Midlands. Note, on the way, Weatheroak Hill, a 1 in 6 (!) climb from the Coach and Horses PH. Fortunately, it's not part of the ride.

Refreshments

Teas at Manor Farm, **Earlswood**
Bell PH, **Tanworth-in-Arden**
Holly Bush PH, **Gorcott Hill**
Coach and Horses Inn,
Weatheroak Hill
Peacock Inn, **Forhill**

Yardley Wood station

Earlswood

The Lakes station

Tanworth-in-Arden

Nearest railway

- Yardley Wood
- Shirley
- Whitlocks End
- Earlswood
- The Lakes
- Wood End

BIRMINGHAM ▶ STRATFORD-UPON-AVON

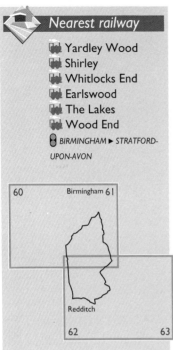

Places of interest

Earlswood Lakes 3
Three reservoirs, with a capacity of 14,000 locks of water, were constructed in 1821 to provide top-up water for the Stratford-upon-Avon canal. They are a great favourite with anglers and sailors of small dinghies. There is also a nature trail in the wood between the lakes and the lane to Earlswood station. At Manor Farm there is a milking shed with viewing area and small craft centre

Tanworth-in-Arden 4
Umberslade Children's Farm contains farm animals, a museum, farm walks, displays and a children's playground. There are picnic areas with cover available when wet and a farm shop selling light refreshments

Beoley 5/6
Beoley (pronounced Bee-ley) was the home of the Sheldon family, who in 1509 introduced tapestry weaving to England. Many of their tapestries were woven at nearby Bordesley and some can be seen in Birmingham University's Barber Institute. A pleasant walk through the churchyard leads to a field (good picnic spot) overlooking Icknild Street

Icknild Street from 6 to 8
More correctly known as Ryknild Street: a Roman (and indeed prehistoric) road between the Cotswolds and the north. It ran from the Fosse Way near Bourton-on-the-Water to outside Sheffield and other routes meet it at Bidford and Lichfield. It served as the main route between Redditch and Birmingham and remained important as a waggoner's route until the railways came 150 years ago

Holt End

Weatheroak Hill

Headley Heath

1 L at exit from Yardley Wood, then L past Trittiford Mill Park onto the dual-carriageway towards Yardley Wood. SA at X-roads after 1 mile 'Majors Green'. At LH bend 1st R '11'9" height and 7.5T weight restrictions'. Under aqueduct and L at T-j, then 1st L and L again at T-j across lift-bridge over Stratford-upon-Avon canal to Drawbridge PH; R at T-j (NS). After sharp LH bend 'Fulford Heath'

2 Cross bridge over railway at Whitlocks End Station, then 2nd L into Birchy Leasowes Lane (NS) and R at T-j (NS) into Dickens Heath Road, then immediately L (NS) into Cleobury Lane, continuing SA at X-roads (NS). R at T-j by Red Lion PH, then L 'Hockley Heath 3¼' at X-roads

3 Immediately R into narrow road running alongside reservoir and then R along lane between two reservoirs; **take care** – single track road, vehicles approaching in both directions and merging from left. Across bridge over M42 and L at T-j 'Wood End, Tanworth 1', then R at T-j onto B4101 'Tanworth 1, Redditch 6' and 1st L 'Tanworth Childrens Farm 1'. Downhill, then climb into Tanworth-in-Arden

➡ **page 63**

7 L Redhill Road at T-j just after passing Peacock Inn, then immediately R Icknild Street and 1st R 'Hollywood, Headley Heath'

8 L at T-j 'Kings Norton', then 1st R by Gay Hill Farm into Dark Lane (NS), 1st L into Crabmill Lane (NS) and R at T-j

9 SA at roundabout by Maypole PH 'Solihull' **take care** busy, fast moving traffic. L at mini-roundabout

10 R at roundabout into School Road, then SA at next roundabout, continuing across narrow canal bridge. L at T-j opposite Trittiford Mill Park and lake, then follow main road round RH bend to return to Yardley Wood station

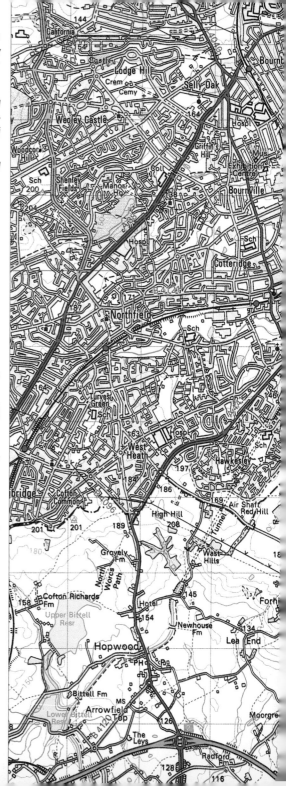

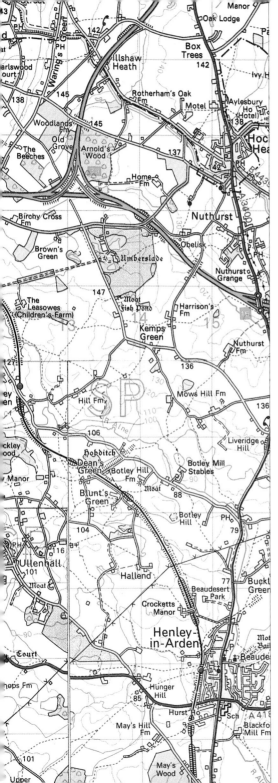

3 Immediately R into narrow road running alongside reservoir and then R along lane between two reservoirs; **take care** – single track road, vehicles approaching in both directions and merging from left. Across bridge over M42 and L at T-j 'Wood End, Tanworth 1', then R at T-j onto B4101 'Tanworth 1, Redditch 6' and 1st L 'Tanworth Childrens Farm 1'. Downhill, then climb into Tanworth-in-Arden

4 1st R in village 'Aspley Heath, Ullenhall 2'. Bates Lane becomes Alderhanger Lane at X-roads after ½ mile; bear L Tanworth Lane (in effect SA) where Alderhanger Lane swings R after further ½ mile, then L at T-j A435 **take care** fast moving traffic and L again up slip-road 'Ullenhall'

5 At offset X-roads at top of slip-road R 'Beoley' across bridge over A435, then L 'No Through Road' (NS). At bottom of hill lane deteriorates into track. **Take care**. L at T-j by The Village PH onto B4101

6 R 'Weatheroak' just after Beoley church into Icknield Street, then 1st L 'Rowney Green' and immediately R into Icknield Street 'narrow road'. Between here and Forhill the surface is poor. Pass under M42 bridge. L at T-j, facing Coach and Horses PH then immediately R 'Forhill, narrow road'

← **page 60**

From Redditch to the relics of a medieval forest and through the Arrow Valley

▲ 16th-century Flemish stained glass in St Peter's church, Abbots Morton

*T*ake the Cross City electric train to Redditch for an enjoyable ride through the peaceful countryside where Warwickshire and Worcestershire meet along the Arrow Valley and down to the River Avon at Bidford. You may choose the route just to take in the scenery and the many small villages with an air of permanence, yet still in the West Midlands commuter belt. Alternatively you may like to see the fine houses of Coughton Court, intimately linked with the Gunpowder Plot, and Ragley Hall. The south-western part of the ride offers a varied scene of mixed farming, a series of attractive settlements and the black and white architecture of Abbots Morton. The landscape around Billesley and Aston The route is very rich in interesting churches, and is most suitable for the Historic Churches Preservation Trust's fund-raising day on the second Saturday of September. Across the county boundary you are in the valleys of the Arrow and its tributary the Alne.

Refreshments

Wheelbarrow Castle PH, **Radford**
Café, Plough Inn, **Bidford**
Cottage of Content PH, **Barton**
Bell Inn, **Welford**
Blue Boar Inn, **Temple Grafton**
Mother Huff Cap PH, **Great Alne**
Tearoom at **Coughton Court**
Green Dragon Inn, **Sambourne**

Redditch   Feckenham   Inkberrow   Abbots Morton   Weethley Gate   Broom

Start

Redditch station

P Redditch

Distance and grade

36 miles

Easy/moderate

Terrain

A mixture of gradients. Ascents and descents, some of them fairly steep but none arduously long, but with many fairly flat sections

Nearest railway

Redditch 🚇 CROSS CITY
LINE: LICHFIELD ▶ BIRMINGHAM
▶ REDDITCH

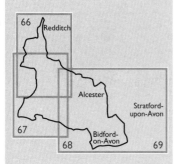

Places of interest

Feckenham 4
A medieval royal manor in the heart of the King's Forest of Feckenham. In the High Street are several well-preserved timber-framed houses, unusually set on high plinths, and later brick houses display the history of vernacular architecture over several centuries

Abbots Morton 9
A village you would think had reached us through a time warp! Black and white houses and cottages packed in (as Pevsner remarks) astonishing variety along a single street make this an attractive diversion from the main road. Lower down is very domestic with cottages sideways-on to the road on long narrow plots. The church, built in the 14th and 16th centuries, has many attractions, including an early 16th-century south window

Ragley Hall (off the route) 9/10
A magnificent 17th-century Palladian mansion a mile and a half north along the A435 from Dunnington Cross. Noted for its elegant baroque plasterwork and fine collections of furniture, paintings and porcelain, with stables and a carriage collection. The 400-acre park (originally laid out by Capability Brown) contains an adventure playground and picnic place

Bidford-on-Avon 11
The chief architectural attraction is the 15th-century bridge. The old fire station behind the church is now a craft shop. A good place for a lunch break is in its old fashioned High Street where there are a chip shop, pubs, bank and tearoom

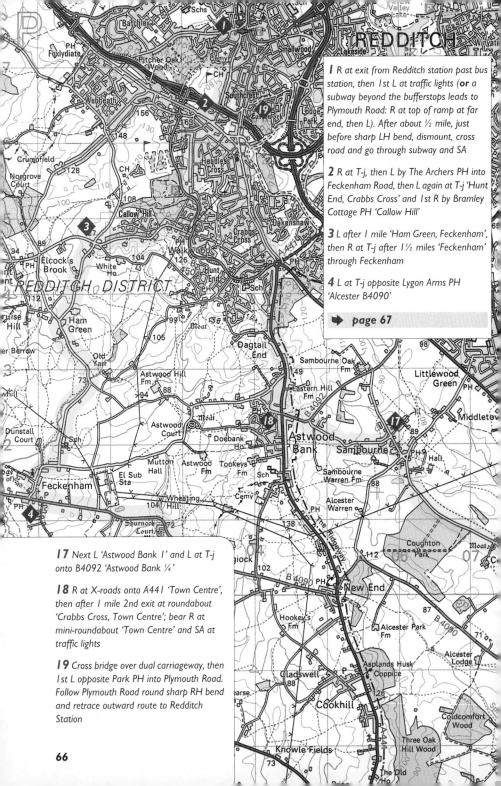

1 R at exit from Redditch station past bus station, then 1st L at traffic lights (**or** a subway beyond the bufferstops leads to Plymouth Road: R at top of ramp at far end, then L). After about ½ mile, just before sharp LH bend, dismount, cross road and go through subway and SA

2 R at T-j, then L by The Archers PH into Feckenham Road, then L again at T-j 'Hunt End, Crabbs Cross' and 1st R by Bramley Cottage PH 'Callow Hill'

3 L after 1 mile 'Ham Green, Feckenham', then R at T-j after 1½ miles 'Feckenham' through Feckenham

4 L at T-j opposite Lygon Arms PH 'Alcester B4090'

➡ **page 67**

17 Next L 'Astwood Bank 1' and L at T-j onto B4092 'Astwood Bank ¼'

18 R at X-roads onto A441 'Town Centre', then after 1 mile 2nd exit at roundabout 'Crabbs Cross, Town Centre'; bear R at mini-roundabout 'Town Centre' and SA at traffic lights

19 Cross bridge over dual carriageway, then 1st L opposite Park PH into Plymouth Road. Follow Plymouth Road round sharp RH bend and retrace outward route to Redditch Station

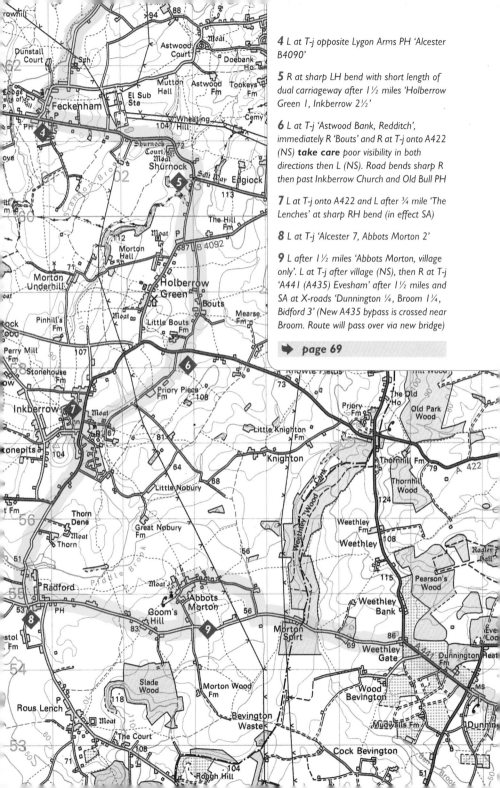

4 L at T-j opposite Lygon Arms PH 'Alcester B4090'

5 R at sharp LH bend with short length of dual carriageway after 1½ miles 'Holberrow Green 1, Inkberrow 2½'

6 L at T-j 'Astwood Bank, Redditch', immediately R 'Bouts' and R at T-j onto A422 (NS) **take care** poor visibility in both directions then L (NS). Road bends sharp R then past Inkberrow Church and Old Bull PH

7 L at T-j onto A422 and L after ¾ mile 'The Lenches' at sharp RH bend (in effect SA)

8 L at T-j 'Alcester 7, Abbots Morton 2'

9 L after 1½ miles 'Abbots Morton, village only'. L at T-j after village (NS), then R at T-j 'A441 (A435) Evesham' after 1½ miles and SA at X-roads 'Dunnington ¼, Broom 1¼, Bidford 3' (New A435 bypass is crossed near Broom. Route will pass over via new bridge)

➡ **page 69**

10 L at T-j 'Wixford 1, Bidford 1, Alcester 3'. R at T-j onto B4085 and continue for 1¼ miles into Bidford. Dismount and cross B439 **take care** to walk along footpath then R 'Buses Only' from westerly direction into High Street

Short cut to Temple Grafton

After turning R into B4085 at instruction 10 1st L 'Ardens Grafton 1¼, Temple Grafton 2¼', then R at T-j 'Ardens Grafton ¾, Temple Grafton 1¼'. L at Golden Cross PH 'Temple Grafton 1', then L again in Temple Grafton 'Haselor ¾, Alcester 3' into Croft Lane and as from instruction 14 of full route

Alternative route into Bidford

As for short route to Golden Cross PH where R 'Bidford 1½' then R at T-j Tower Hill 'B439 Evesham' and L at bottom of hill 'Buses Only' sign only applies to traffic from opposite direction. A longer route but has fines views across the Avon Valley

11 In Bidford L at X-roads by Anglo Saxon PH over narrow bridge, then L after ¾ mile 'Barton ½, Welford 3¼'

12 L at T-j in Welford, then cross river and R at T-j onto B439, then L 'Binton ½'

13 L by Blue Boar Inn after 1½ miles 'Temple Grafton ¾, Ardens Grafton 1¼, Bidford 4'

14 Climb hill, then R by church and school 'Haselor 1¾, Alcester 3'. After steep drop SA across A46 at X-roads beside octagonal Toll Bar Cottage 'Haselor ¾, Great Alne 1½' **take care** busy trunk road and through Haselor, then SA at X-roads 'Great Alne 1, Studley 5¾' and cross River Alne

15 L at T-j by old station house 'Alcester B4089' and follow road sharp L past Mother Huff Cap PH on RH side in Great Alne, then 1st R 'Coughton 2 via ford'. The water at the ford is deep: use footbridge

16 R at T-j by Coughton Court R onto A435, L 'Sambourne 1½, Astwood Bank 3', then L in Sambourne 'Astwood Bank 1½' and SA at X-roads by Green Dragon Inn 'Astwood Bank'

◀ **page 66**

From King's Norton across valley heads to Huddington

The full route is a treasure house of delights, offering splendid views on fine days from many high vantage points. A wonderful outdoor museum at Avoncroft has restored a range of domestic architecture from the past six centuries. South-west of Birmingham the hills have always presented a natural barrier to transport and on the ride you see a history of the engineering solutions to this problem. The route itself has been carefully designed to take you down the steeper hills! Along the canal, boats are likely to be locking through the longest flight in the country. There is no need to ride the complete route on a single day. The ride to Avoncroft and back on one day may be complemented by another ride beginning at Barnt Green or Bromsgrove and reaching out to Himbleton and Radford on a second day.

Refreshments

Peacock PH, **Forhill** Café at **Burcot Garden Centre** Tearoom, **Avoncroft Museum of Historic Buildings** Queen's Head PH, **Stoke Pound** Tearoom at **Hanbury Hall** Galton Arms PH, **Himbleton** Boot Inn, **Flyford Flavell** Bird In Hand PH, **Stock Wood** Red Lion PH, **Bradley Green** Coach and Horses PH, **Weatheroak Hill**

Start

King's Norton station.

Alternative starts for riders arriving by car: Forhill Countryside Centre (small car park closes early); along Hewell Road at Barnt Green; public car park adjoining the Dragoon PH beside Bromsgrove station

P King's Norton station

Distance and grade

Maximum 55 miles, with many shorter routes possible

Moderate

Terrain

Between King's Norton and Bromsgrove there is much high ground, one notable climb goes up Aqueduct Lane. South of Avoncroft and on the return route the sharper climbs are short as a rule.

King's Norton · Lea End · Hopwood · Finstall · Whitford Bridge · Piper's Hill · Broughton Green · Shell · Himbleton · Huddington

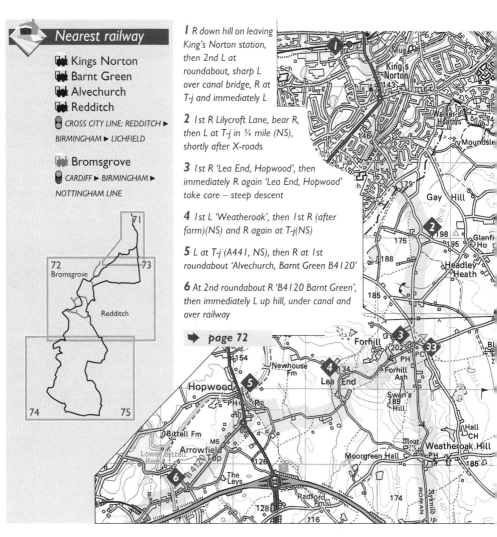

Nearest railway

🚉 Kings Norton
🚉 Barnt Green
🚉 Alvechurch
🚉 Redditch

🔵 CROSS CITY LINE: REDDITCH ▶
BIRMINGHAM ▶ LICHFIELD

🚉 Bromsgrove

🔵 CARDIFF ▶ BIRMINGHAM ▶
NOTTINGHAM LINE

1 R down hill on leaving King's Norton station, then 2nd L at roundabout, sharp L over canal bridge, R at T-j and immediately L

2 1st R Lilycroft Lane, bear R, then L at T-j in ¾ mile (NS), shortly after X-roads

3 1st R 'Lea End, Hopwood', then immediately R again 'Lea End, Hopwood' take care – steep descent

4 1st L 'Weatheroak', then 1st R (after farm)(NS) and R again at T-j(NS)

5 L at T-j (A441, NS), then R at 1st roundabout 'Alvechurch, Barnt Green B4120'

6 At 2nd roundabout R 'B4120 Barnt Green', then immediately L up hill, under canal and over railway

➡ **page 72**

33 T-j L Redhill Road 'West Heath, Northfield', then immediately R Icknield Street 'King's Norton' and retrace outward route to King's Norton station

7 L at T-j (NS), across M42, then immediately R 'Coopers Hill'

A (From Barnt Green station) joins here: leave station on east side, then R at T-j into main street, 1st L, SA at X-roads and under railway bridge to meet main route just before M42 crossing

8 After 1 mile, R at T-j 'Tardebigge, Bromsgrove' for 1½ miles, bearing R (road narrows and descends under railway)

9 L at B4096 T-j, then immediately R Pikes Pool Lane 'Narrow Road'

10 R at T-j 'Bromsgrove 1¼', then immediately L at T-j 'Aston Fields ¾', R again at T-j 'Droitwich Worcester' and immediately L

11 SA at X-roads 'No Through Road'. In or after rain, R at X-roads at instruction 11, then 1st L Upper Gambolds 'Bentley' and join canal at canal bridge, continuing downhill

B (From Bromsgrove station) joins here: R at X-roads at top of station approach, then R 'Primrose Hospice', continuing to X-roads at instruction 11; in or after rain, 2nd R Upper Gambolds 'Bentley'

(beside Finch End Farm after sharp LH bend) **not** 1st R Lower Gambolds 'No Through Road' and join canal at canal bridge

12 At canal bridge R onto towpath and walk for 1¼ miles (riding bicycles on the towpath is prohibited; give way to anglers and to canal users locking boats through)

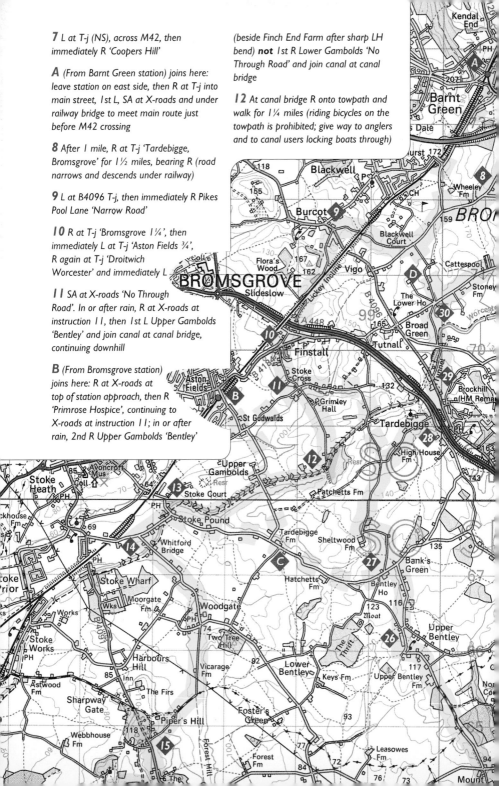

13 Leave towpath at Queen's Head PH, then to visit Avoncroft Museum: R for 1 mile on leaving towpath, then L into Museum just before T-j with A38. Return to Queen's Head PH by same route. **Or** if not visiting Avoncroft: L and bear R Stoke Pound Lane (alternatively continue walking along towpath from Queen's Head PH under three overbridges and L up narrow path immediately after 3rd bridge. R onto Whitford Bridge Lane (NS) and SA at X-roads by Gate Hangs Well PH in instruction 14)

C After L at canal bridge, 1st L 'Bentley', then after 1¼ miles bear L 'Webheath, Redditch' and L 'Tardebigge' after further ¼ mile to rejoin long route at point 27

14 1st L immediately after row of houses (Farfield) Whitford Bridge Lane 'Woodgate', then SA at X-roads by Gate Hangs Well PH 'Dodderhill Common, Hanbury'

15 L at T-j with main road B4091 (NS), then R at offset X-roads 'Droitwich' (NT signpost: 'Hanbury Hall')

➡ *page 75*

26 After 1 mile bear R and immediately L Banks Green 'Webheath, Redditch', then L again at T-j towards Stoke Pound

27 Immediately R Sheltwood Lane 'Tardebigge' and R 'Tardebigge, Bromsgrove' at T-j, then after 1¼ miles bear R High House Lane. If returning to Bromsgrove

station do **not** bear R into High House Lane but L at this junction 'Finstall', then L at T-j Dusthouse Lane (NS) SA at X-roads at Stoke Cross (instruction 11 on outward route), bear R where Dusthouse Lane becomes St Godwald's Road, L at T-j and L again at BR 'Bromsgrove' sign into station approach

28 R at T-j 'Redditch 3', bear L under dual carriageway, then L 'Burcot' at T-j B4096

29 1st R 'Alvechurch', then L at T-j 'Lickey End, Bromsgrove', over canal and immediately R 'Blackwell, Barnt Green'

30 At X-roads R 'Alvechurch, Rowney Green' (after 1¼ miles hump back bridge at foot of steep hill before LH bend **take care**)

D SA Agmore Lane at X-roads at instruction 30, R at T-j 'Barnt Green, Alvechurch', then 1st L 'Barnt Green, Birmingham' to foot of station drive in 1¼ miles

31 At T-j L 'A441 Birmingham' (**NB** not present A441, which is crossed as you begin to climb The Holloway), then immediately R 'Rowney Green, Inkford' and SA at top of hill 'Portway, Beoley' (**not** L into village)

32 1st L 'Icknield Street, Narrow Road' (just before T-j), then SA at offset X-roads 'Forhill, Narrow Road' Icknield Street 'Narrow Road', rejoining outward route at Peacock PH

⬅ *page 71*

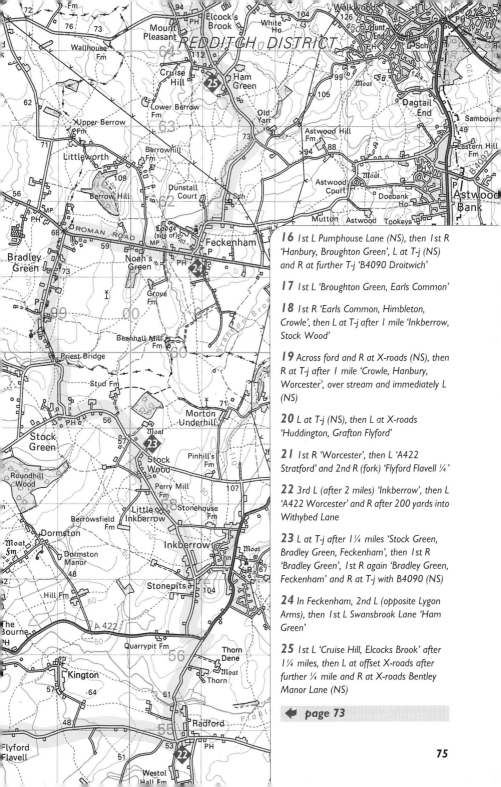

16 1st L Pumphouse Lane (NS), then 1st R 'Hanbury, Broughton Green', L at T-j (NS) and R at further T-j 'B4090 Droitwich'

17 1st L 'Broughton Green, Earls Common'

18 1st R 'Earls Common, Himbleton, Crowle', then L at T-j after 1 mile 'Inkberrow, Stock Wood'

19 Across ford and R at X-roads (NS), then R at T-j after 1 mile 'Crowle, Hanbury, Worcester', over stream and immediately L (NS)

20 L at T-j (NS), then L at X-roads 'Huddington, Grafton Flyford'

21 1st R 'Worcester', then L 'A422 Stratford' and 2nd R (fork) 'Flyford Flavell ¼'

22 3rd L (after 2 miles) 'Inkberrow', then L 'A422 Worcester' and R after 200 yards into Withybed Lane

23 L at T-j after 1¼ miles 'Stock Green, Bradley Green, Feckenham', then 1st R 'Bradley Green', 1st R again 'Bradley Green, Feckenham' and R at T-j with B4090 (NS)

24 In Feckenham, 2nd L (opposite Lygon Arms), then 1st L Swansbrook Lane 'Ham Green'

25 1st L 'Cruise Hill, Elcocks Brook' after 1¼ miles, then L at offset X-roads after further ¼ mile and R at X-roads Bentley Manor Lane (NS)

◀ **page 73**

From Droitwich to Great Witley and back down the wonderful Teme Valley

*T*he very best time to ride this route is in the spring, when the apple blossom is out. The view from the top of the Abberley Hills, just before descending to Stanford Bridge, is stunning: the valley full of apple orchards with the Welsh hills as a backdrop. This route is also suitable for taking part in the Historic Churches Preservation Trust's sponsored ride in September. Before the Abberley Hills the route detours to take in the burnt-out shell of Witley Court. The return takes in some very narrow and quiet Worcestershire lanes and a stretch of stony farm track. The route may be shortened by leaving the main route soon after Great Witley and rejoining it at Ockeridge. However, this means missing out on the gloriously scenic part of the route along the Teme Valley.

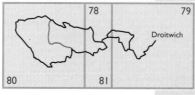

Start

Droitwich Station
P Pay-and-display in town centre

Distance and grade

37 miles (29 miles with short cut)

Moderate/strenuous

Terrain

The route is mostly along undulating, often deeply rural, lanes. Several hills but the route mostly goes down the steeper ones. 100 foot (30 m) climbs up from Holt Fleet to Holt Heath and from Great Witley on the outward leg; 250 foot (83 m) climbs from Ham Bridge across the Teme up to Martley and from Holt Fleet to Uphampton on the return

Nearest railway

Droitwich
WORCESTER ► KIDDER-MINSTER ► BIRMINGHAM

Droitwich   Ombersley Holt Fleet   Shrawley   Structon's Heath   Great Witley Kingswood Common Stanford Bridge

Droitwich 1

The town has seen many changes, from a medieval centre of industry to today's overspill dormitory town. 'Wich' (the

Domesday name) means a place of salt. Salt was produced here from pre-Roman till early modern times. The burning of timber to boil the brine was largely responsible for the disappearance of the surrounding Forest of Feckenham. In the 1840's the industry moved to Stoke Works, nearer Bromsgrove, the town becoming a fashionable spa

Witley Court 6/7

A Georgian mansion frequented by royalty which fell into ruin after being partly destroyed by fire in 1937. Now restored, you may wander through remains of

▲ *Droitwich town centre: a swing bridge over the Droitwich Canal*

once sumptuous halls. Immediately R of the house and resembling a large shed from the outside is Great Witley Church, the baroque interior of which has to be seen to be believed

Refreshments

Bowling Green Inn, **Hadley**
Good pubs in **Ombersley**
Lenchford Hotel, by river at **Shrawley**
Villa Fiore tea rooms, **Witley Court**
Hundred House PH, **Great Witley**
Bridge Hotel, **Stanford Bridge**
Crown PH, **Martley**
Fruiterers Arms PH, **Uphampton**
Plenty of choice in **Droitwich**

Woodbury Hill

(short cut) 7 to 10
A stone age fort on a hilltop near Great Witley; during the English Civil War the 'Clubmen', who banded together for self-defence against either side, met here in March 1645

Ham Bridge Martley Northingtown Farm Holt Fleet Uphampton Hadley

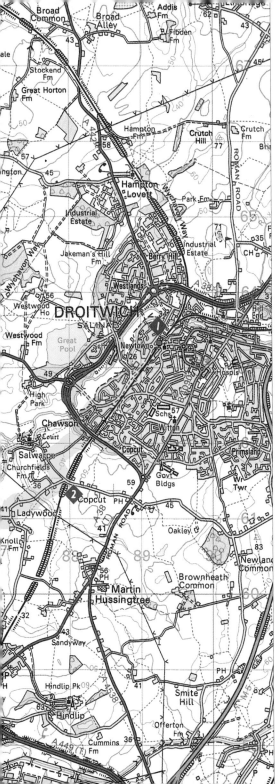

1 Bearing R Union Lane to T-j with Ombersley Way, where R, then L at roundabout after railway bridge 'Ombersley, Tenbury A4133'. L New Chawson Lane and L at T-j 'Martin Hussingtree, Worcester A38'

2 R 'Ladywood, Fernhill Heath', then R again 'Porter's Mill, Hadley' and bear R after canal bridge 'Hadley'

3 R at X-roads after 1¼ miles 'Sinton' **easy to miss**, dismount at T-j with A449 and cross road by way of metalled path over central reservation **take care**, then through chicane barrier, down footpath and R onto old road into Ombersley

4 L at roundabout in Ombersley 'Tenbury A4133', crossing River Severn at Holt Bridge

5 R at T-j in Holt Heath onto A443 and immediately R again 'Stourport B4196, Shrawley 2, Astley 4', then L after 1¼ miles 'Sankyns Green, Great Witley 4'

➡ **page 80**

11 R at T-j at end of concrete road (A443), then 1st L 'Holt Church' and between sand pits. After church keep L past new houses, then R at T-j (A4133) downhill to cross River Severn again at Holt Bridge

12 2nd L 'Boreley' at top of hill, then 2nd R (NS) to Uphampton, bearing R 'Ombersley' (ignore 1st R). Fruiterers' Arms PH is L, then R, both in village

13 After ½ mile L at T-j, immediately R 'Hadley', R across A449 **take care**, then L 'Hey Lane only' and L again after 1 mile by old barn, lane then bends to R, R at T-j with A4133 (NS) and immediately L 'Hadley, Martin Hussingtree'

14 L at T-j to return to Droitwich by reverse of outward route (ignore signpost R 'Droitwich' just before Salwarpe village turn)

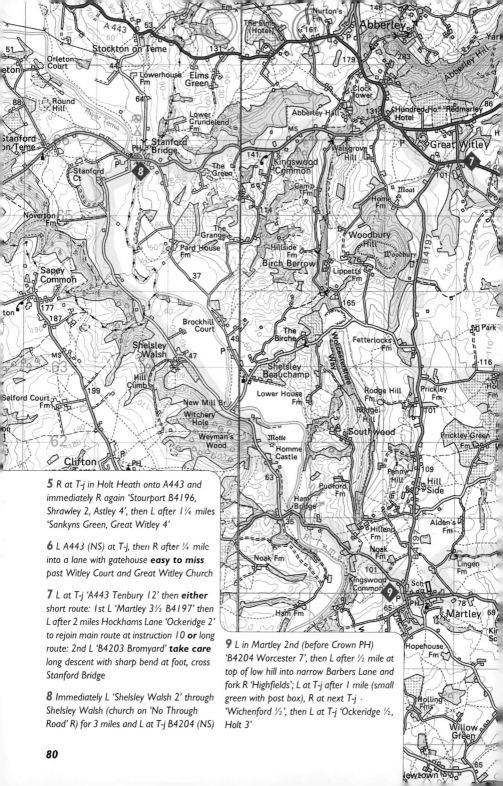

5 R at T-j in Holt Heath onto A443 and immediately R again 'Stourport B4196, Shrawley 2, Astley 4', then L after 1¼ miles 'Sankyns Green, Great Witley 4'

6 L A443 (NS) at T-j, then R after ¼ mile into a lane with gatehouse **easy to miss** past Witley Court and Great Witley Church

7 L at T-j 'A443 Tenbury 12' then **either** short route: 1st L 'Martley 3½ B4197' then L after 2 miles Hockhams Lane 'Ockeridge 2' to rejoin main route at instruction 10 **or** long route: 2nd L 'B4203 Bromyard' **take care** long descent with sharp bend at foot, cross Stanford Bridge

8 Immediately L 'Shelsley Walsh 2' through Shelsley Walsh (church on 'No Through Road' R) for 3 miles and L at T-j B4204 (NS)

9 L in Martley 2nd (before Crown PH) 'B4204 Worcester 7', then L after ½ mile at top of low hill into narrow Barbers Lane and fork R 'Highfields'; L at T-j after 1 mile (small green with post box), R at next T-j 'Wichenford ½', then L at T-j 'Ockeridge ½, Holt 3'

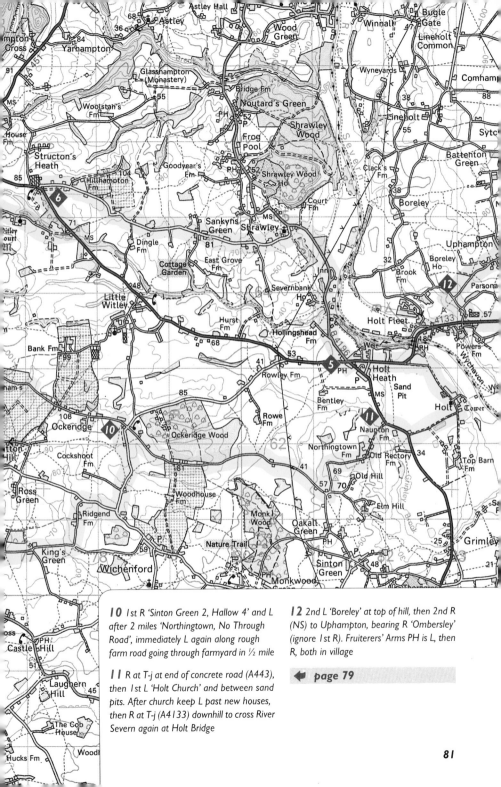

10 1st R 'Sinton Green 2, Hallow 4' and L after 2 miles 'Northingtown, No Through Road', immediately L again along rough farm road going through farmyard in ½ mile

11 R at T-j at end of concrete road (A443), then 1st L 'Holt Church' and between sand pits. After church keep L past new houses, then R at T-j (A4133) downhill to cross River Severn again at Holt Bridge

12 2nd L 'Boreley' at top of hill, then 2nd R (NS) to Uphampton, bearing R 'Ombersley' (ignore 1st R). Fruiterers' Arms PH is L, then R, both in village

◀ page 79

13 From Longbridge across the Lickey Hills to Dodford and the Clent Hills

Ten miles from Birmingham's city centre the Clent and Lickey Hills stand like sentinels protecting the countryside of Worcestershire from an encroaching conurbation. The route over the Lickey Hills offers superb views, weather permitting, south-west across the mid-Worcestershire plain to the distinctively shaped Malvern Hills. Housman's 'blue remembered hills' (the family lived just south of the route at Fockbury) lie on the western horizon in Shropshire. This is a pleasantly open, gently undulating landscape in which to cycle. Over the Clent Hills, later in the day, the landscape changes again. Narrow, often sunken, lanes make their way up and down delightful valleys and around Walton Hill before returning past Waseley Hill Country Park to suburbia.

Start

Longbridge or Barnt Green station

🅿 Hewell Road, Barnt Green (to east of station) or on-road in Fiery Hill Road (to west of station)

Distance and grade

35 miles (32 miles with short cut)

Moderate/strenuous

Terrain

The start and finish, over the Lickey and Clent Hills, are fairly challenging. Some of the steeper climbs may be avoided by starting from Barnt Green. The middle section in the Worcestershire Plain is gently undulating

Nearest railway

🚆 Longbridge
🚆 Barnt Green
⭕ CROSS CITY LINE: REDDITCH ▶ BIRMINGHAM ▶ LICHFIELD

84

85 Birmingham

86

87

Longbridge

Cofton Hackett

Lickey

Lydiate Ash

Upper Catshill

Dodford

Cooksey Green

Rushock

Lickey Hills 3/4

The hills have outcrops of very ancient rock among the woods, heath and open spaces. There are splendid views from the indicator, near Beacon Hill car park, north across

the city and south across the Severn Valley and into Wales (weather permitting). Lickey Hills Country Park Visitor Centre is down the lane behind the 19th-century Holy Trinity church. Bromsgrove's manor courts used to meet here and there was a gibbet in the days of the highwayman

Dodford 6

The site of an isolated pre-reformation Augustinian priory

▲ *Standing stones on Clent Hill*

where the Chartist land colony was founded by Fergus O'Connor in 1848

Clent Hills 12/14

Walton Hill, at 1,036 feet (315 m) is the nearest point over 1,000 feet (305 m) high to the West Midlands conurbation. To climb it, follow the footpath at the top of a steep climb out of Upper Clent village. The four standing stones on the summit of Clent Hill to the north are not prehistoric but one of several follies near Hagley Hall, products of mid-18th century romanticism

Refreshments

Limited opportunities en route, so a packed lunch is a good idea
Lickey Hills Visitor Centre, **near Lickey church**
Crown PH, **Catshill**
Gate Inn PH, Nailers' Arms PH, **Bournheath**
Dodford Inn, **Dodford**
Swan PH, Talbot PH, **Chaddesley Corbett**
Talbot PH, Old Horseshoes PH, **Belbroughton**

Waseley Hill 14

A pleasant country park with an excellent visitor centre

Chaddesley Corbett   Hillpool   Drayton   Belbroughton   Clent   Rumbow Cottages   Dayhouse Bank

1 L at exit from Longbridge station, after ¼ mile R Coombs Lane at X-roads, R Groveley Lane at T-j B4096, then L at T-j

2 2nd L Chestnut Drive and SA along bridlepath where road turns sharp R. R at T-j with metalled road (NS but gateposts to Cornerstone on L), then L Kendal End Road at T-j with B4120 and 1st R beside Barnt Green Inn

3 Sharp R at X-roads into Twatling Road. SA at X-roads over B4096 by Lickey Church (**take care**), L at T-j 'Bromsgrove' and R at X-roads (NS)

4 SA at offset X-roads, then L at T-j 'Bromsgrove 3 A38' and 1st R Woodrow Lane (**take care**: A38 is very busy), R at T-j by village hall, then L Wildmoor Lane at T-j and 1st R Church Road

5 R at T-j by church B4091 'Stourbridge', then over M5 and 1st L 'Bournheath', SA at X-roads and SA at offset X-roads

6 R at T-j, then 1st L Priory Road, R at T-j by house with initials 'BSB', then SA at X-roads across A448

 page 86

➡ page 86

Short route

1st R after Belbroughton village Dark Lane, across A491 **take care** and R past Hollybush PH, then immediately L Gorse Green Lane; fork R 'Bell Heath, Fairfield', then 1st L 'Romsley, Halesowen' after rejoining main route at end of Shutt Mill Lane and continue from instruction 13

11 After 1 mile R Summerfield Road, R again at T-j (NS), then L at T-j with dual carriageway A491 (NS) and immediately R (**take care**) 'Walton Pool', 1st L 'Clent, Romsley'

12 R at X-roads 'Romsley, Halesowen' and after 1 mile uphill R by High Harcourt Farm 'Walton Hill' at St Kenelm's Pass, then bear R at fork, R again at sharp LH bend (in effect SA) 'No Motorbicycles or Cars Except for Access'

13 R at T-j at Rumbow Cottages, R again at fork, then L at T-j 'Bell Heath, Fairfield' (ignore earlier L turn with same signposting), 1st L 'Romsley, Halesowen', then R at X-roads 'Bell Heath, Fairfield' and 2nd L at five-armed X-roads 'Frankley, Rubery' Quantry Lane

14 L at T-j B4551 'Romsley, Halesowen', then almost immediately R 'No Through Road', follow lane sharp R and L across motorway, bear L past farm buildings, L at top of rise and R at T-j. Keep SA

15 After 2 miles fork R at brow of hill with pylon conspicuous beyond, immediately R at T-j, R at mini-roundabout and SA across A38 to return to Longbridge station. If going on to Barnt Green, follow instructions 1 and 2 (Hewell Lane is 1st R under railway bridge in Kendal End Road, Fiery Hill Road on R immediately before bridge) or take train for Redditch (Barnt Green is the next station)

6 R at T-j, then 1st L Priory Road, R at T-j by house with initials 'BSB', then SA at X-roads across A448

7 R at T-j 'Droitwich', then 1st R 'Kidderminster' between open field and house and R at T-j 'Kidderminster, Woodcote Green', 1st L Cooksey Green Lane, then R at T-j 'Rushock, Kidderminster' past Badge Court

8 L at T-j (NS), then 1st R (NS), R at T-j in Rushock, past church and down hill, then R again at T-j (NS); bear R (in effect SA) at three-way junction, bear R again at fork. Bear L at T-j with A448

9 R into Chaddesley Corbett village 'Drayton, Belbroughton' and 1st L (after crossing stream) 'Stourbridge, Narrow Road', SA at X-roads 'Hillpool', then 1st R 'Hillpool, Narrow Road' through hamlet and R again at T-j 'Drayton' and L at T-j in Drayton Village

10 L at T-j 'Belbroughton, Stourbridge', R at T-j B4188 (in effect SA) and continue SA at Talbot PH through Belbroughton village towards Clent

← page 85

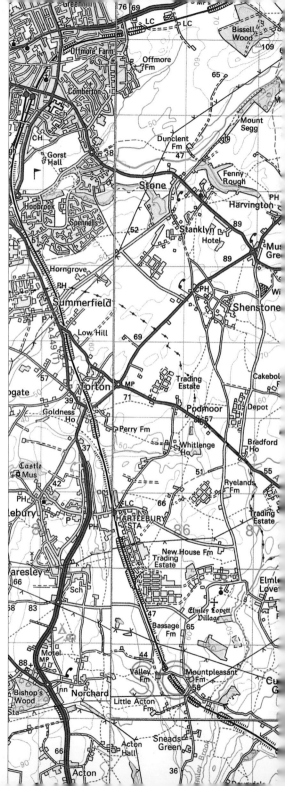

14 From Longbridge by winding country lanes to old centres of agricultural industry and ancient woods

Start

Longbridge station
Alternative start from
Beacon Hill car park
(between 11/12)

P None near
Longbridge station.
Beacon Hill car park in
Monument lane

A marvellous, delightful ride, ideal for
beginners or for a Sunday afternoon. It
begins by slipping through a gap between the
Lickey and Waseley Hill into the peaceful
Worcestershire countryside. A brief climb
over the southern edge of the Clent Hills gives
panoramic views across the Worcestershire
Plain with the Shropshire Hills and the
Malverns beyond,
before dropping
down through
some deliciously
wooded lanes to
Belbroughton.

Distance and grade

32 miles (short cut
16 miles)
Moderate

Terrain

The starting and
finishing stretches
traverse the hills to the
southwest of the
conurbation. The fringe
of the Worcestershire
Plain is undulating but
never strenuous.
Eastern parts of the
route are hillier: there
are three steep hills but
you go down the
steepest

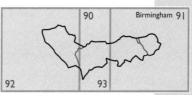

	90	Birmingham 91
92	93	

From Belbroughton to the village of
Bluntington the route is less hilly and more
open. The section of the route through
remnants of the Forest of Feckenham is
particularly beautiful, with the opportunity
of strolls through Chaddesley or Pepper
Woods. The final stage up over the Lickey
Hills affords further panoramic views across
Birmingham towards the Trent Valley.

Nearest railway

 Longbridge CROSS
CITY LINE: REDDITCH ▶
BIRMINGHAM ▶ LICHFIELD

 Blakedown
 WORCESTER ▶ STOURBRIDGE
▶ BIRMINGHAM

Longbridge

Dayhouse Bank

Bell Heath

Belbroughton

Broome

Churchill

Churchill 6

A quiet, unspoilt hamlet with brick buildings and sandstone rock-face; a yew tree here is estimated to be 1,000 years old

Churchill Forge 6

There used to be 12 water mills in the square mile around the church; now only one remains. Tools such as scythes, spades and forks were forged here and sharpened by using the power from the two waterwheels

Harvington Hall
(off the route) 7/8

A picturesque and irregular Elizabethan moated manor house, the medieval timber framed building was given a brick casing by the Pakingtons who owned it in Tudor times. There are priest's holes and links with the Gunpowder Plot families

▲ *Harvington Hall*

Chaddesley Wood 8

250 acres of ancient woodland, now a nature reserve, with a number of rights of way through them. The main timber is broad-leaf – oak, birch and hazel coppice

Refreshments

There are not many shops or pubs en route so a packed lunch may be a wise idea

*Teas and light meals, **Waseley Hill Country Park***

*Light refreshments and full meals, **Harvington Hall***

*Talbot PH, Old Horseshoes PH, **Belbroughton***

*Swan PH, **Fairfield***

*Tea and light meals, **Lickey Hills Visitor Centre***

Pepper Wood 9

130 acres of ancient woodland owned and managed by The Woodland Trust as a community woodland. A part is given over to traditional coppicing

Woodrow   Woodcote Green   Fairfield   Upper Catshill   Lydiate Ash   Lickey

1 R out of Longbridge station and immediately R Tessall Lane. Walk 'wrong' way along one-way street for a short stretch to bridge over stream. SA across A38 **take care** and at mini-roundabout bear L uphill, then 2nd L and L again at T-j. Continue past Waseley Hill Country Park on L, cross M5 and bear L downhill 'Old House Lane'

Short route

To start from Beacon Hill car park. L out of car park along Monument Lane, then L 'Rednal ¾, Birmingham 9 B4096' at X-roads with B4096, L at roundabout and L again (just after Hare and Hounds PH) for 1 mile, across Bristol Road South **take care**: dual carriageway, separated by A38 on overbridge, then L Cock Hill Lane, L again at T-j after ½ mile into Cross Farms Lane, past Waseley Hill Country Park, over M5 into Old House Lane and then follow main route from instruction 2

2 L at T-j, then immediately R 'Belbroughton, Stourbridge'

3 2nd R 'Hollies Hill, Walton Hill', then R at A491 T-j **take care** and immediately L 'Hollies Hill'

4 L at T-j through Belbroughton and follow B4188 for 1 mile after village, then R 'Private Road to The Park and Red Hall, Bridle Path only' and follow drive round

➡ **page 92**

8 After 2 miles sharp L back on yourself at T-j 'Dordale, Belbroughton', then R at T-j 'Catshill, Bromsgrove'

9 After 1¼ miles, L Brook Lane 'Fairfield', then L at T-j with B4091 'Stourbridge' and 1st R opposite Swan PH 'Wildmoor'

10 R at T-j, then under motorway and 1st L Cobnall Lane, L at T-j Woodrow Lane, R at T-j with A38 'Bromsgrove 2¾' and walk up footpath from bus bay to turn L at end (A38 is a very busy road: **take care**)

11 1st R Alvechurch Highway, then L up hill at X-roads and 1st R 'Barnt Green' (**NB** adjoining Beacon Hill car park)

12 L Rose Hill 'Rednal ¾, Birmingham 9 B4096' at X-roads with B4096, SA at roundabout, 5th R (between two parts of Rover plant), 2nd L and L at X-roads Longbridge Lane to return to Longbridge station

3 2nd R 'Hollies Hill, Walton Hill', then R at A491 T-j **take care** and immediately L 'Hollies Hill'

4 L at T-j through Belbroughton and follow B4188 for 1 mile after village, then R 'Private Road to The Park and Red Hall, Bridle Path only' and follow drive round

Short cut to Bournes Green

L Drayton Road 'Chaddesley Corbett' at end of Belbroughton village, where B4188 curves sharp R, L 'Bournes Green, Bromsgrove' in Drayton opposite shop and L at T-j (NS) after 1¼ miles to rejoin main route and go on to instruction 8

5 L at T-j past Broome church on R, L at next T-j, SA across two X-roads (1st with A450 'Churchill, Kidderminster', 2nd with A456 'Churchill'), L at T-j Stakenbridge Lane 'Churchill, Cookley, Wolverley' then R under railway bridge

6 At X-roads L 'Blakedown', then 1st R 'Wolverley, Bridgnorth'

7 After 1 mile, L just before A451 junction. After further mile at A456 L, then immediately R, R again and then L (in effect SA) **take care** 'Bluntington, Paintball Games', SA at A450 X-roads and SA after 1 mile at X-roads 'Woodcote Green, Bournes Green'

8 After 2 miles sharp L back on yourself at T-j 'Dordale, Belbroughton', then R at T-j 'Catshill, Bromsgrove'

9 After 1¼ miles, L Brook Lane 'Fairfield', then L at T-j with B4091 'Stourbridge' and 1st R opposite Swan PH 'Wildmoor'

◀ **page 91**

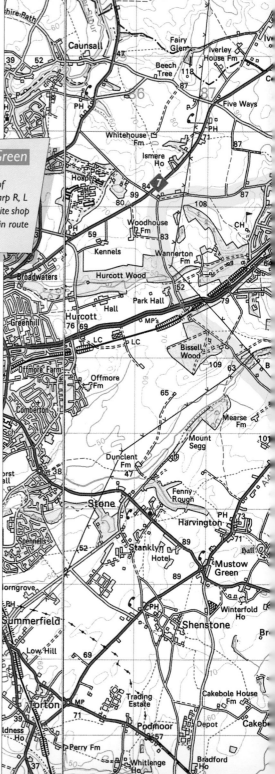

15 From Stourbridge to a sandstone outcrop, and a river-powered ferry

The Wyre Forest used to extend much further than it does today. This route dips and bobs its way through land that was once, and is still reminiscent of, the Wyre Forest. As you drop down to the Stour, look out for the pine-covered, sandstone outcrop of Kinver Edge. From Romsley there are fine views of the Severn Valley and central Shropshire before you descend to the ferry. A lack of road bridges has left this reach of the Severn relatively unspoilt and remote. Beyond the Severn you can either skirt the Shropshire mining village of Highley or explore hillier ground in sight of the Clee Hills.

Refreshments

Unicorn PH, Lion Inn **Hampton Loade**
Bell PH, **Alveley**
Fox and Hounds PH, **Stottesdon** (just off the route)
Harbour PH, **Upper Arley**
Plough and Harrow PH, Old Plough Inn, tea rooms, fish and chip shop in **Kinver**

Start

Stourbridge Junction station

P As above

Distance and grade

45 miles (shorter route 42 miles, 28 miles using Severn Valley Railway)

Moderate/strenuous (the short route A is easy/moderate)

Terrain

The route is mainly flat or downhill to the River Severn. It has a steep climb to Sutton where you can choose between the Kinlet route which has one hill and the ride to Bagginswood which takes in three. There is a steep climb out of the Severn Valley from Upper Arley, whether you cycle the whole route or take the Severn Valley Railway train

▶ The Severn Valley Railway

Stourbridge   Whittington   Kinver   Hartsgreen   Birdsgreen   Hampton Loade   Sutton   Chor

Nearest railway

🚃 Stourbridge
Junction 🚶 *WORCESTER ▶*
STOURBRIDGE ▶ BIRMINGHAM

🚃 Hampton Loade
🚃 Arley 🚶 *SEVERN VALLEY*
RAILWAY (SUMMER ONLY)

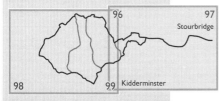

Places of interest

Kinver Edge and Holy Austin Rock *6/7*
The Edge is a series of sandstone outcrops worth climbing for the extensive views and has a 7-acre Iron Age hill fort on top. The cave dwellings at Nanny's Rock and Holy Austin Rock may be Celtic and were occupied until the 1940's

Hampton Loade *13*
The foot ferry is the last remaining of three that existed between Bridgnorth and Bewdley. The ferry is connected to an overhead wire and the ferrywoman merely sets the rudder and the current powers the boat. There is a small fare (bicycle included)

Severn Valley Railway *from 13 to 23*
Opened in 1862, the line used to run 40 miles alongside the Severn from Shrewsbury to Hartlebury Junction near Stourport. It closed in the 1960's but enthusiasts managed to save the 12½ mile stretch between Bridgnorth and Bewdley

◀ *The ferry at Hampton Loade*

1 L from Stourbridge Junction station into car park, then L into Brook Road at small roundabout. Under two railway bridges, up to traffic lights at X-roads with A491 and SA Heath Lane

2 SA at 1st roundabout and immediately bear R at 2nd roundabout South Road

3 SA at 3rd roundabout by cemetery Dunsley Road, bearing L where minor road on R goes SA

4 SA at X-roads with A449 after 2 miles into cul-de-sac **take care**. Go past barns and across footbridge, then bear R following bridlepath past cottage. Cross river to Anchor Hotel and bear L where lane joins housing estate to continue on Dark Lane

5 R at T-j by The Cross PH, then L at T-j 'Enville 2¾, Bobbington 6½' and into Kinver

6 L past Old Plough Inn 'Kinver Edge ½, Wolverley 3¼'. Pass Holy Austin Rock

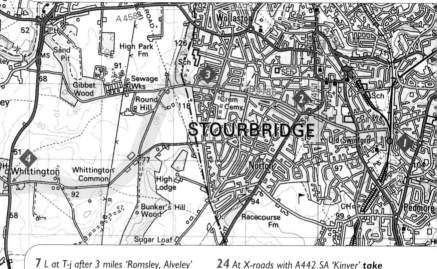

7 L at T-j after 3 miles 'Romsley, Alveley'

8 R at T-j after 1 mile 'Romsley ¾, Alveley 3'. Within ½ mile pass under arching oak trees to crest hill where R into narrow lane. **Take care** poor surface often muddy. At T-j by cottage R (in effect SA). Downhill and through farm. L up tree-lined lane at T-j

9 R at T-j towards bench seat and telephone box, and SA for 1¼ miles

Short route

A To remain east of River Severn. At T-j go L away from telephone box, then L after ½ mile at T-j with A442 and immediately L 'Kinver'. Follow main route instructions from instruction 24

➡ page 98

24 At X-roads with A442 SA 'Kinver' **take care**

25 At X-roads after 3½ miles R 'Kinver 1½' and enter Kinver

26 In Kinver R at T-j by Old Plough Inn and through village. At far end of High Street, on LH bend, R (in effect SA) 'Caunsell, Cookley, Churchill', then 1st L Dark Lane, bearing R on LH left bend to Anchor Hotel

27 From far LH corner of Anchor Hotel car park R into private road / bridle path and cross River Stour. Pass cottage, cross Staffordshire and Worcestershire Canal via narrow humpback bridge, then SA at X-roads with A449 – **take care** and retrace outward route to Stourbridge Junction station (at roundabout by Mary Stevens Park keep R and go up Mount Street)

9 R at T-j towards bench seat and telephone box, and SA for 1¼ miles

10 R at T-j in sight of A442

11 L immediately after crossing bridge over stream and as road bends L around the hill R onto track. **Take care** very poor surface

12 L at T-j in ¾ mile after sharp bend, then downhill towards A442. At X-roads with A442 SA into track **take care**, then R at T-j of tracks, L at T-j with road, then downhill to river

13 At bottom of hill R into car park at sharp LH bend. Foot ferry landing stage is on far LH of car park. After crossing the river leave landing area through gate and L into road. Climb steep hill past SVR station

14 L at T-j with B4555 in Sutton, then choice of longer or shorter West of Severn routes. For the longer route, via instructions 15 to 18, R after 150 yards. For the shorter route, via instructions 19 and 20, continue on B4555

Longer route

15 L at T-j after 1½ miles onto B4363, then 1st R 'Chorley 1¾, Stottesdon 3½'

16 L after Chorley 'Harcourt, Bagginswood, Cleobury Mortimer'. Bagginswood is ½ mile SA

17 L at T-j 'Kinlet, Cleobury Mortimer, Bewdley' through Bagginswood and SA for about 2½ miles

18 L at T-j with B4363 'Highley, Bridgnorth, Bewdley', then after ¼ mile 2nd R (fork) onto B4199. Continue from instruction 21

Shorter route

19 After ¾ mile 1st R just past house on R 'Borle Mill, Kinlet'. Steep, **take care**. Cross narrow bridge over Borle Brook. At T-j with B4555 R (in effect SA) 'Kinlet, Cleobury Mortimer, Bewdley' and after good ½ mile L at T-j with B4194 'Kinlet 2, Cleobury Mortimer 6½, Bewdley 8'

20 In Kinlet village by PH on corner L 'Bewdley 5½, Kidderminster 8½' B4194

21 At T-j with B4194 L 'Bewdley 5, Kidderminster 8, Buttonbridge ½, Buttonoak 2½'. Continue along B4194 through Wyre Forest for 2 miles after Buttonbridge

22 In small hamlet L just after telephone box 'Pound Green ½, Arley 1½, No Through Road', and bear R just past New Inn **steep descent**, crossing narrow bridge over SVR. Just past Harbour Inn dismount and bear R, crossing River Severn by footbridge

23 On reaching road bear R uphill

← **page 97**

Short cut

B Via Severn Valley Railway. After crossing the Severn at instruction 13, go L at exit from landing stage and up steep hill under railway. Immediately after bridge L into station entrance. **Take extreme care** when crossing railway line. Take train to Arley. From Arley station: L at end of station drive downhill past Harbour PH and bear R to recross Severn by footbridge. Continue from instruction 23

The ferry at Hampton Loade may not operate during flooding after heavy rain

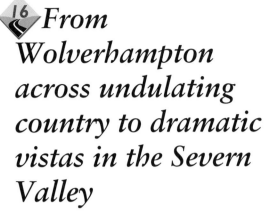

16 *From Wolverhampton across undulating country to dramatic vistas in the Severn Valley*

The scenery of East Shropshire is very different from that of the counties further east. Here are low tree-covered hills and deeply cut valleys. The route takes you to places which well merit a visit: the beautiful village of Worfield; the Severn Valley Railway; the precious pedestrian ferry at Hampton Loade. Several breathtaking vistas come into view, including the spectacular drop into the Severn Valley. Here the Severn is dominated by the two-tier town of Bridgnorth, standing on its sandstone ridge. The section from Bridgnorth to Hampton Loade can be covered by steam train (check times). After the steep climb out of the Severn Valley the return to Wolverhampton is by way of quiet lanes via Tuckhill and Claverley.

Start

Wolverhampton station

P Multi-storey car park in Piper's Row (R on town centre side of ring road off Bilston Street)

Distance and grade

55 miles (but may be shortened)

///// Moderate

Terrain

The full distance of 55 miles is a real challenge: it requires a long summer day and low gears but short cuts are suggested, including using the steam train to reduce the distance by 5 miles and cut out a steep climb. The eastern section is mainly flat, whilst the western section contains the deep valley of the River Severn into which the route drops and climbs twice

Wolverhampton   Wightwick Manor   Pattingham   Chesterton   Dallicott   Worfield   Bridgnorth   Eardingr

🚂 Wolverhampton
🔵 *LOCAL SERVICES (NOT SUNDAY MORNINGS)* 🔵 *INTERCITY SERVICES*

🚂 Bridgnorth
🚂 Hampton Loade
🔵 *SEVERN VALLEY RAILWAY (SUMMER ONLY)*

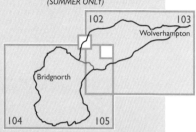

Places of interest

Bridgnorth 11
Full of sights worth seeing, you will find a wealth of material to divert you and occupy your time. Victorian cliff railway (will not take your bicycle but they will watch it for you!). The caves at top of the Cartway were occupied until 1856 and the castle still remains surrounded by many fine buildings from various centuries

Claverley 17
All Saints' church is a notable edifice in red sandstone. The exterior looks all of one piece but the interior reveals works by William the Conqueror's half-brother Roger de Montgomery (who died in 1094) down to restoration in 1902, including a 15th-century porch and upper tower and a 17th-century hammer beam roof. Most noteworthy is the 12th- or 13th-century wall paintings uncovered during 20th-century restoration

Refreshments

Many pubs along the route Plenty of choice of teashops and pubs in **Bridgnorth High Town** *Railwaymans Arms PH,* **SVR Bridgnorth station** *Unicorn PH, Lion Inn,* **Hampton Loade**

▲ *Bratch Bottom Lock on the Staffordshire and Worcestershire Canal at Claverley*

elmarsh

Hampton Loade

Tuckhill

Claverley

Upper Aston

Seisdon

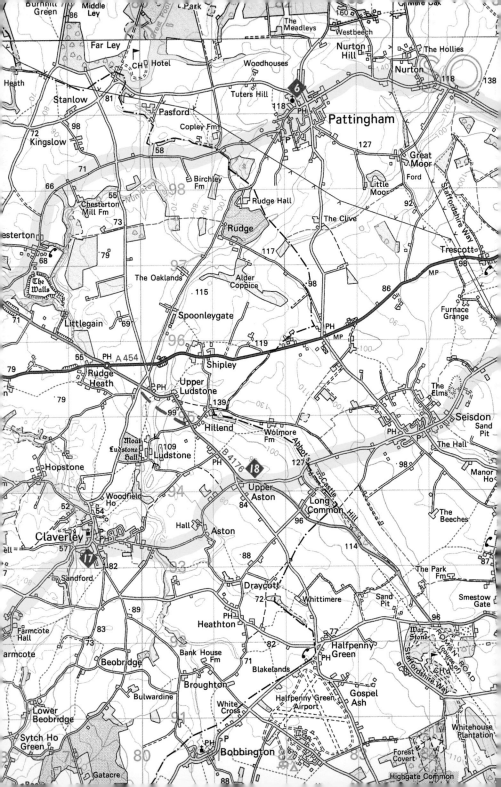

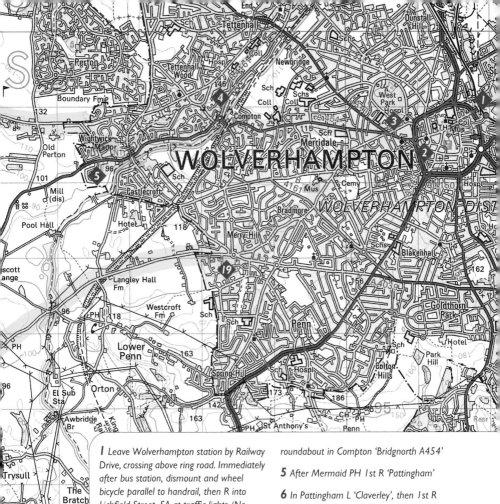

1 Leave Wolverhampton station by Railway Drive, crossing above ring road. Immediately after bus station, dismount and wheel bicycle parallel to handrail, then R into Lichfield Street. SA at traffic lights (No Motor Vehicles), then SA at mini-roundabout SA (Bicycles, Taxis, PSVs only) and continue SA through 2 more sets of traffic lights

2 At ring road roundabout stay in A41 lane and leave after low office block, in effect SA, 'Whitchurch A41' and 'Bridgnorth A454'. Can also dismount and use subway. Pass church with spire

3 At 3-way forks use middle lane for A454 'Bridgnorth, Compton'. Pass to R of Eye Infirmary

4 Under old railway bridge after 1½ miles (Sustrans route to Stourbridge), then L at roundabout in Compton 'Bridgnorth A454'

5 After Mermaid PH 1st R 'Pattingham'

6 In Pattingham L 'Claverley', then 1st R Chesterton Rd 'Copley'. SA at X-roads 'Chesterton'. On through village and L at T-j then immediately R 'Unsuitable for Heavy Vehicles'

➡ **page 104**

17 R at T-j by Kings Arms in Claverley, then bear L at fork. After 2 miles SA at X-roads

18 immediately R onto B4176. 1st L up to White Tinkers Castle. On through Seisdon

19 After 5 miles, Merry Hill roundabout, SA Trysull Road. At traffic lights SA Bradmore Road. R at T-j, follow 'Town Centre' and reverse of outward route from Chapel Ash to return to Wolverhampton station

7 At T-j in Hilton R 'Bridgnorth A454' and immediately L Sandpit Lane. R after 200 yards on bridleway, then grassed track and into field. Exit by white gate L on drive from Dallicott House. At road R

8 R onto A454 and immediately L 'Worfield', then bear L at T-j. After ½ mile R into village. L past church (steep up to T-j), then R (opposite Old Vicarage Hotel) and 1st L

9 After 1 mile, L at X-roads 'Rindleford'. Descend to sharp bend at derelict mill. SA on narrow footpath R of mill, to footbridge. Up narrow lane to T-j, then L 'Bridgnorth, Enville'

10 R at roundabout 'Bridgnorth'. Descend to 2nd roundabout where L 'Town Centre'. Immediately R 'Low Town' and over River Severn. Bear L, then L again B4363 'Cleobury Mortimer' where route bears sharp R

11 On B4363 1st L 'Eardington, Chelmarsh'. SA along B4555. After Eardington 1st R 'Astbury' (narrow lane)

12 R at T-j and immediately L (narrow lane NS) into Chelmarsh. L at T-j by church onto A4555. After ¾ mile 1st L 'Hampton Loade, River Severn'. R at T-j through Hampton and descend to station

13 At lane's end, through field gate to ferry. Press bell on pole to R of ferry and wait for attendant (small charge). Up lane SA from river

14 R at T-j 'Kidderminster A442'. 1st L 'Coton, Kingsnordley'. L and immediately R bear R at fork (NS) and SA at X-roads up narrow lane into Tuckhill

15 L at T-j. Track 1st L leads to Tuckhill church, set in amazing ancient trees. Then 1st R (NS) and L at T-j 'Bridgnorth A458'

16 1st R (halfway down hill) 'Claverley'. Bear R at X-roads 'Claverley' (not sharp R). SA at 1st T-j, then L to Farmcote. SA at staggered X-roads to Claverley

17 1st R by Kings Arms in Claverley and immediately L at T-j. After 2 miles SA at X-roads and immediately R onto B4176

◀ **page 103**

The ferry at Hampton Loade may not operate during flooding after heavy rain

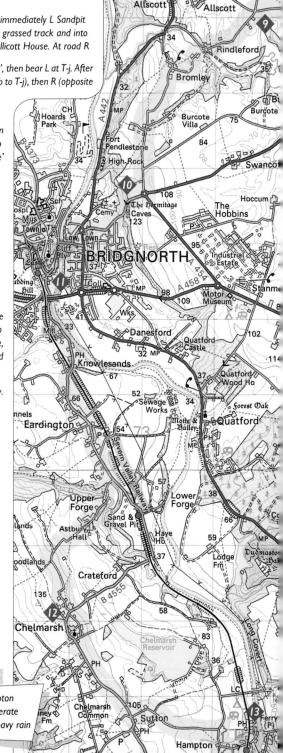

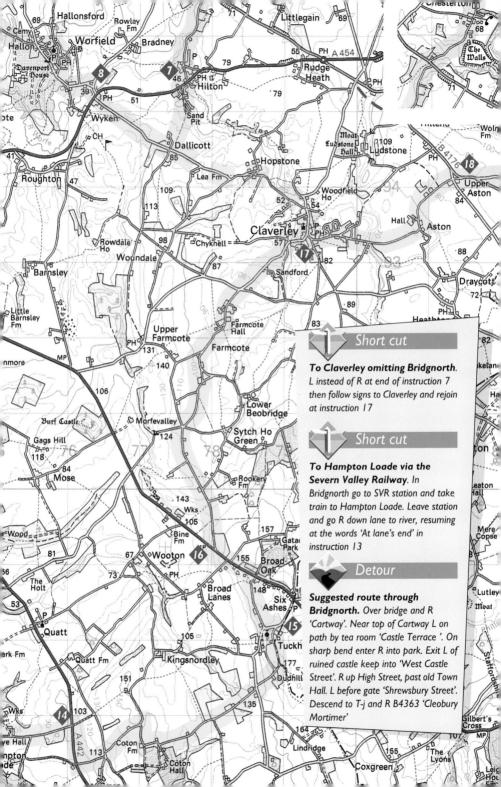

⬆ Short cut

To Claverley omitting Bridgnorth. L instead of R at end of instruction 7 then follow signs to Claverley and rejoin at instruction 17

⬆ Short cut

To Hampton Loade via the Severn Valley Railway. In Bridgnorth go to SVR station and take train to Hampton Loade. Leave station and go R down lane to river, resuming at the words 'At lane's end' in instruction 13

▲ Detour

Suggested route through Bridgnorth. Over bridge and R 'Cartway'. Near top of Cartway L on path by tea room 'Castle Terrace'. On sharp bend enter R into park. Exit L of ruined castle keep into 'West Castle Street'. R up High Street, past old Town Hall. L before gate 'Shrewsbury Street'. Descend to T-j and R B4363 'Cleobury Mortimer'

From Wolverhampton to the cradle of the Industrial Revolution

The outward leg of this ride is through upland sheep pasture and remote scattered villages. Badger with its tranquil pools and Beckbury above the River Worfe are good places for a pause. Once across the A442 there is the sheer visual exhilaration of the Severn Gorge: first the far bank shrouded in dense woodland, then – with the sudden descent – a rooftop view of the valley's industrial hamlets. The valley bottom offers a heady mix of intimacy on a domestic scale and bold engineering structures in a spectacular natural setting. As you may not have time to see the various museums at one go, the ticketing allows you to return on successive visits. The homeward journey lies

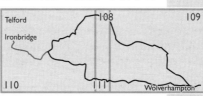

through larger villages: the church at Tong is particularly worth a visit. The solitary cyclist could spend more time exploring the Severn Gorge, and then ride just to Albrighton for the train back to Wolverhampton.

Start

Wolverhampton station

P Multi-storey car park in Piper's Row

Distance and grade

42 miles

🏔🏔🏔 Moderate

Terrain

A good day's ride across the easy, undulating countryside of north-east Shropshire. Two escarpments may well require walking: the climbs from Compton to Wightwick Bank and out of the Severn Gorge. The descent into Coalport on this route could be dangerous in frosty conditions

Wolverhampton

Pattingham

Badger

Beckbury

Brock

▶ The iron bridge at Ironbridge

▼ Ironbridge, a view of the Severn Gorge from the bridge

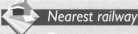

Nearest railway

 Wolverhampton
🚊 INTERCITY SERVICES 🚊 LOCAL SERVICES

🚊 **Albrighton**
🚊 **Codsall**
🚊 **Bilbrook**
🚊 WOLVERHAMPTON ▶ SHREWSBURY

Refreshments

Crown PH, **Pattingham** *Seven Stars PH,* **Beckbury** *Refreshments at most of the Ironbridge Gorge museums Tea shops,* **Coalport** *and* **Ironbridge** *Restaurant in the Roses and Shrubs Nursery where the route turns into* **Albrighton** *Chip shops at* **Albrighton** *and* **Cosford**

Places of interest

Ironbridge Gorge 12
The birthplace of the Industrial Revolution, where in 1709 Abraham Darby first smelted iron with coke instead of charcoal. As well as the iron bridge itself, the world's first iron rails, wheels, boat and high pressure steam engine were built here. The Gorge also became a centre for the manufacture of ceramics, with porcelain at Coalport and tiles at Jackfield. Nowadays there are ten museums spread along a four mile length of the Gorge

Cosford (just off the route) 17
The Aerospace Museum at RAF Cosford, has displays of civil and military aircraft

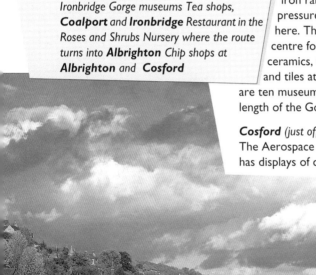

nberton Brimstree Hill Tong Albrighton Codsall

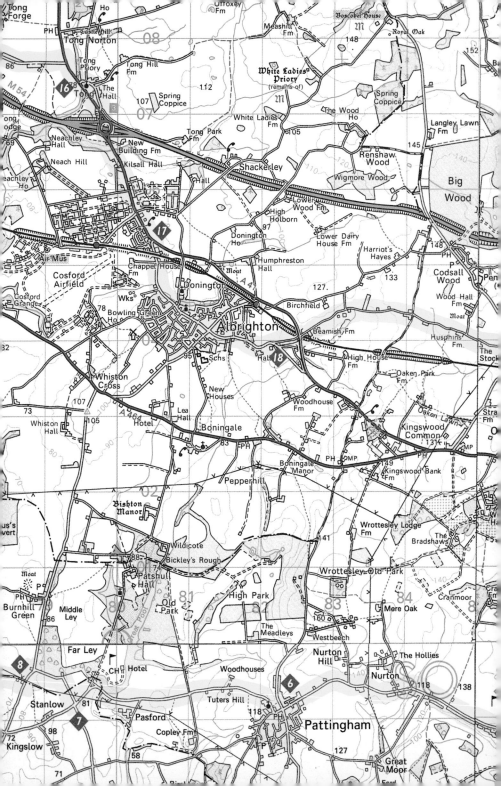

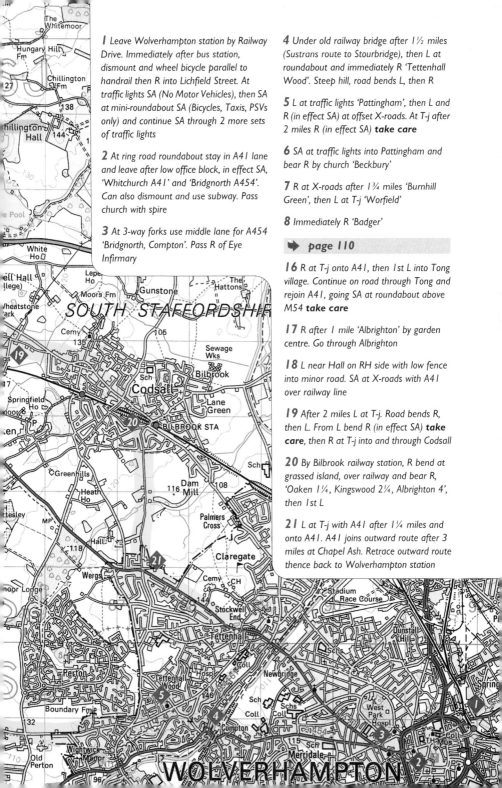

1 Leave Wolverhampton station by Railway Drive. Immediately after bus station, dismount and wheel bicycle parallel to handrail then R into Lichfield Street. At traffic lights SA (No Motor Vehicles), then SA at mini-roundabout SA (Bicycles, Taxis, PSVs only) and continue SA through 2 more sets of traffic lights

2 At ring road roundabout stay in A41 lane and leave after low office block, in effect SA, 'Whitchurch A41' and 'Bridgnorth A454'. Can also dismount and use subway. Pass church with spire

3 At 3-way forks use middle lane for A454 'Bridgnorth, Compton'. Pass R of Eye Infirmary

4 Under old railway bridge after 1½ miles (Sustrans route to Stourbridge), then L at roundabout and immediately R 'Tettenhall Wood'. Steep hill, road bends L, then R

5 L at traffic lights 'Pattingham', then L and R (in effect SA) at offset X-roads. At T-j after 2 miles R (in effect SA) **take care**

6 SA at traffic lights into Pattingham and bear R by church 'Beckbury'

7 R at X-roads after 1¾ miles 'Burnhill Green', then L at T-j 'Worfield'

8 Immediately R 'Badger'

➡ *page 110*

16 R at T-j onto A41, then 1st L into Tong village. Continue on road through Tong and rejoin A41, going SA at roundabout above M54 **take care**

17 R after 1 mile 'Albrighton' by garden centre. Go through Albrighton

18 L near Hall on RH side with low fence into minor road. SA at X-roads with A41 over railway line

19 After 2 miles L at T-j. Road bends R, then L. From L bend R (in effect SA) **take care**, then R at T-j into and through Codsall

20 By Bilbrook railway station, R bend at grassed island, over railway and bear R, 'Oaken 1¼, Kingswood 2¼, Albrighton 4', then 1st L

21 L at T-j with A41 after 1¼ miles and onto A41. A41 joins outward route after 3 miles at Chapel Ash. Retrace outward route thence back to Wolverhampton station

7 R at X-roads after 1¾ miles 'Burnhill Green', then L at T-j 'Worfield'

8 Immediately R 'Badger'

9 At T-j in Badger R 'Ryton, Beckbury'

10 In Beckbury keep L past Seven Stars PH

11 R at T-j with B4176 after 2 miles, then 2nd exit from roundabout (in effect R) onto A442 **take care**

12 (For Ironbridge Gorge: L ½ mile on L at X-roads 'Coalport'. **Take care**. Museums along both sides of River Severn for 2½ miles and up side valleys R.) R at X-roads 'Brockton' and in Brockton L at T-j with B4379

13 1st R 'Kemberton' (within sight of A-road) and L at T-j into Kemberton. Follow the road through the village. Cross river at Evelith hamlet

14 ½ mile after Evelith sharp L at T-j, then 1st R after 500 yards, SA at X-roads with A464 and over railway line

15 R at T-j and under M54. Road then widens **watch out** for speeding motorists

16 R at T-j onto A41, then 1st L into Tong village. Continue on road through Tong and rejoin A41, going SA at roundabout above M54 **take care**

 page 109

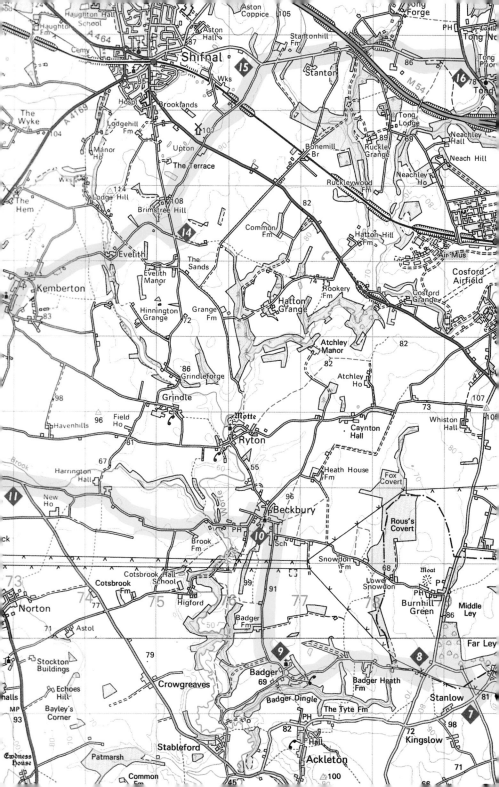

18 *From Wolverhampton to Charles II's hiding place through intriguing villages and 18th-century parkland*

Start

Wolverhampton station

P Multi-storey car park in Piper's Row
Alternative, without cycling on urban roads: Codsall station

P Station Road, Codsall

Distance and grade

30 miles from Wolverhampton (27 with short cut)
22 miles (full route) from Codsall
✎ Easy

Terrain

A leisurely route for the less energetic, with little in the way of major climbs, but some busy urban roads which may be cut out by starting from Bilbrook or Codsall station

A ride across old landed estates of south Staffordshire, passing notable country mansions and remnants of ancient woodland. From Wolverhampton the route passes majestic houses along the Tettenhall Road, village green atmosphere at the Rock, and spacious parks, before turning down a sunken lane towards Codsall. An undulating straight run leads to Brewood (pronounced Brood) with its attractive market place. Then the short route heads west to Boscobel past the redbrick 'Black Ladies', while the longer one crosses the old Watling Street and on along undisturbed back lanes to Wheaton Aston, where the Shropshire Union Canal is crossed at a busy place for leisure boating. Boscobel offers fine open views west towards the Wrekin and an optional rapid descent to the ruins of 'White Ladies'. After Chillington there is the choice, at Pendeford, of taking to the canal towpath for the final stretch into Wolverhampton as an alternative to the busy A449.

Wolverhampton   Codsall   Ackbury Heath   Brewood   Horsebrook

Wolverhampton
LOCAL SERVICES   INTERCITY SERVICES

Bilbrook
Codsall
WOLVERHAMPTON ►
SHREWSBURY

Wolverhampton

Refreshments

Plenty of pubs, Passiflora tearoom, **Brewood**
The Bell PH, at A5 X-roads just before **Stretton**
Hartley Arms PH, Coach and Horses PH, **Wheaton Aston**
New Inn PH, on short route just past **Oakley**

Places of interest

Brewood 6

A medieval village rich in history with an attractive market place. Speedwell Castle, a large scale Gothick folly with ogee windows and doorway was built from the winnings of a bet on the Duke of Bolton's horse, Speedwell, in 1750. The village centre has retained much of its Georgian character

Boscobel House 9

A 16th-century hunting lodge once set in dense forest which was a hiding place of Charles II on his escape from the battle of Worcester in 1651

White Ladies Priory 9

Ruins of a small late 12th-century cruciform church less than a mile from Boscobel

Chillington Hall 10

An 18th-century mansion set in spacious estate owned by the Gifford family. The park and lake were laid out by Capability Brown in 1770 but earlier long avenues survive. Halfway along Lower Avenue (now abandoned) is Telford's 1826 canal bridge and there is a four mile signed walk around the lake

▲ Avenue Bridge, over the Shropshire Union Canal at Brewood

Wheaton Aston   Bishops Wood   Gunstone   Oxley

1 Leave Wolverhampton station by Railway Drive. Immediately after bus station, dismount and wheel bicycle parallel to handrail, then R into Lichfield Street. At traffic lights SA (No Motor Vehicles), then SA at mini-roundabout SA 'Bicycles, Taxis, PSVs only' and continue SA through 2 more sets of traffic lights

2 At ring road roundabout stay in A41 lane and leave after low office block, in effect SA, 'Whitchurch A41' and 'Bridgnorth A454'

3 At 3-way forks use RH lane for A41, keep on Tettenhall Lane 'A41 Whitchurch' and SA at X-roads after 1½ miles, still 'A41 Whitchurch'

4 R after 1 mile Keepers Lane (main road bends L) for 1½ miles, then R at T-j

5 L at X-roads 'Codsall, Codsall Wood', then R at X-roads with traffic lights 'Brewood, Coven'. After ¼ mile SA at offset X-roads 'Brewood, Coven'

➡ *page 117*

11 After 100 yards dismount at junction with Ryefield, take the footpath parallel with main road across old canal bridge, R after bridge and follow canal. At next bridge SA main footpath and L after ½ mile. Continue to Autherley Junction, R 'Stourport', L at next canal bridge and follow 2½ miles to Wolverhampton, leaving canal at Broad Street over bridge (near to ring road and Wolverhampton station), then R, across ring road and L, then L again into Station Drive. Otherwise, R at road, then L at roundabout 'Wolverhampton Town Centre'. R at T-j with A449 onto Stafford Road 'Wolverhampton' and follow main road SA over 4 roundabouts

12 After 2½ miles SA at X-roads with ring road. **Take care**: avoid getting stuck in wrong lane. L at mini-roundabout onto Broad Street, then R at traffic lights 'Station' and follow Railway Drive to Wolverhampton station

6 After 3 miles cross canal, then L at X-roads 'Brewood, Penkridge, Bishops Wood' into Brewood, R after church into market place, then L at T-j 'Bishops Wood'. 2nd R Bargate Lane, 1st L onto Horsebrook Lane, then L at T-j with A5 after 1½ miles and immediately R 'Lapley, Church Eaton' into Stretton. **Take care** at R turn across A5 dual-carriageway

Short cut

From Brewood to Bishops Wood. L over Shropshire Union Canal, then SA through Kiddemore Green. Bear L at fork and L again at X-roads to join main route. Continue from instruction 9

7 L at X-roads 'Wheaton Aston, Lapley, Church Eaton', L again after 1½ miles into Wheaton Aston and through village

8 L at T-j and SA across A5 after 1½ miles at offset X-roads 'Bishops Wood, Codsall' to Boscobel House

9 After Boscobel, 1st L 'Coldham, Chillington'. After 1 mile road bends sharp R then follow twisting road past Chillington Hall on R

10 1 mile after hall R onto bridleway 'No Through Road' and 'No Vehicles Access Only' on gate. Cross M54 motorway on bridle bridge. L at T-j in Gunstone by mock Tudor House, SA at X-roads 'Coven, Pendeford' and after 1¼ miles R at T-j 'Bilbrook, Codsall'. After 500 yards R at T-j then L after works and after 700 yards L onto The Driveway

← page 114

19 From Stafford to Butter Hill, along the Shropshire Union Canal to High Offley then Eccleshall

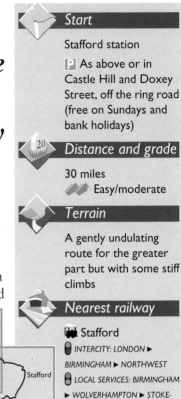

Start

Stafford station

P As above or in Castle Hill and Doxey Street, off the ring road (free on Sundays and bank holidays)

Distance and grade

30 miles

Easy/moderate

Terrain

A gently undulating route for the greater part but with some stiff climbs

Nearest railway

Stafford

INTERCITY: LONDON ▶ BIRMINGHAM ▶ NORTHWEST

LOCAL SERVICES: BIRMINGHAM ▶ WOLVERHAMPTON ▶ STOKE-ON-TRENT

A medium length route with a wide and changing vista of gently rolling countryside, often by way of twisting and dipping lanes across brook or canal. A steep climb out of Stafford is rewarded by splendid views from Butter Hill: Cannock Chase to the south and across to Stafford Castle on its mound to the north. The delightful villages of Bradley and Church Eaton come soon after, with ancient churches of soft red stone. Between Gnosall and rambling Norbury Junction the route is never far from the Shropshire Union Canal but the climb of the day is to High Offley, perched at a height of 433 feet (132 m) and presiding over the spreading patchwork landscape. The scene becomes more domesticated past Bishop's Offley with the woodland and pools of Offley Rock and Mere Pool. After the modest dignity of Eccleshall the route runs across remote hill pasture before dropping to Norton Bridge and Izaak Walton's Cottage. The final leg to Stafford fords Gamesley Brook at Seighford but there is also a footbridge.

Stafford

Coppenhall

Bradley

Church Eaton

Gnosall Heath

Bradley 4

The church is mainly late 13th and early 14th century with a Norman font. This is an attractive setting, next to a pub and looking out onto the countryside

Eccleshall 12

The town's most obvious feature is arcaded frontages along the High Street. Holy Trinity is claimed to be one of the most perfect 13th-century churches in Staffordshire. Eccleshall Castle, a sandstone mansion built in 1695, is just north of the town and in the 20 acres of wooded grounds are ruins of a medieval castle, the residence of the Bishops of Lichfield for 1000 years

 Refreshments

Red Lion PH, **Bradley**
Royal Oak PH, **Church Eaton**
Royal Oak PH, The Horns PH, **Gnosall**
Measham Tea Pot, Junction Inn, **Norbury Junction**
Star PH, Copmere End, overlooking **Cop Mere**
Plenty of teashops and pubs, **Eccleshall**
Mill PH, **Worston**

Izaak Walton's Cottage 13

Walton, author of 'The Compleat Angler', owned this black and white cottage of typical 17th-century domestic architecture. There are displays on Walton's literary and social life and on the history and development of angling. There is also a 17th-century herb garden and picnic orchard

Stafford 1

If you have time to spare after returning to Stafford, there are several places worth visiting. The tourist information office can be found in Ancient High House on Greengate Street, the largest timber framed town house in England, dating from 1595. Stafford Castle, an early Norman earth and timber fortress, can be found a mile to the west of the town on the A518. Returning through the suburb of Doxey a visit can be made to the Doxey Marshes Nature Reserve. On Lichfield Road is an art gallery showing contemporary arts and crafts

High Offley

Bishop's Offley

Eccleshall

Izaak Walton's Cottage

Great Bridgeford

Seighford

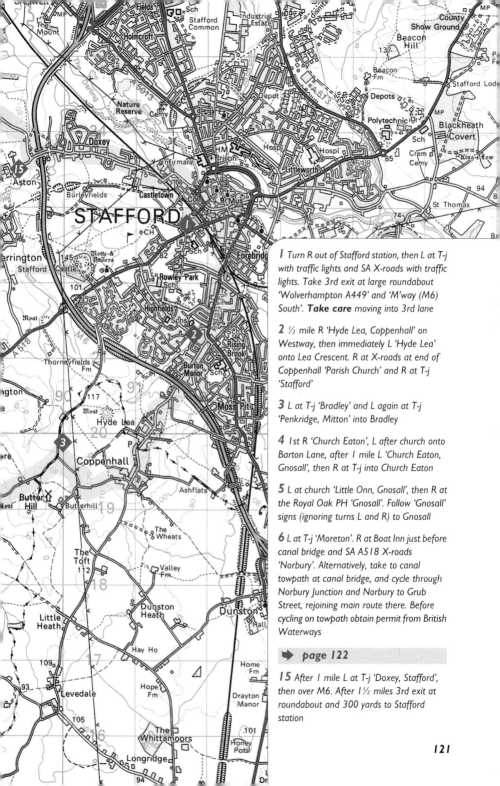

1 Turn R out of Stafford station, then L at T-j with traffic lights and SA X-roads with traffic lights. Take 3rd exit at large roundabout 'Wolverhampton A449' and 'M'way (M6) South'. **Take care** moving into 3rd lane

2 ½ mile R 'Hyde Lea, Coppenhall' on Westway, then immediately L 'Hyde Lea' onto Lea Crescent. R at X-roads at end of Coppenhall 'Parish Church' and R at T-j 'Stafford'

3 L at T-j 'Bradley' and L again at T-j 'Penkridge, Mitton' into Bradley

4 1st R 'Church Eaton', L after church onto Barton Lane, after 1 mile L 'Church Eaton, Gnosall', then R at T-j into Church Eaton

5 L at church 'Little Onn, Gnosall', then R at the Royal Oak PH 'Gnosall'. Follow 'Gnosall' signs (ignoring turns L and R) to Gnosall

6 L at T-j 'Moreton'. R at Boat Inn just before canal bridge and SA A518 X-roads 'Norbury'. Alternatively, take to canal towpath at canal bridge, and cycle through Norbury Junction and Norbury to Grub Street, rejoining main route there. Before cycling on towpath obtain permit from British Waterways

➡ **page 122**

15 After 1 mile L at T-j 'Doxey, Stafford', then over M6. After 1½ miles 3rd exit at roundabout and 300 yards to Stafford station

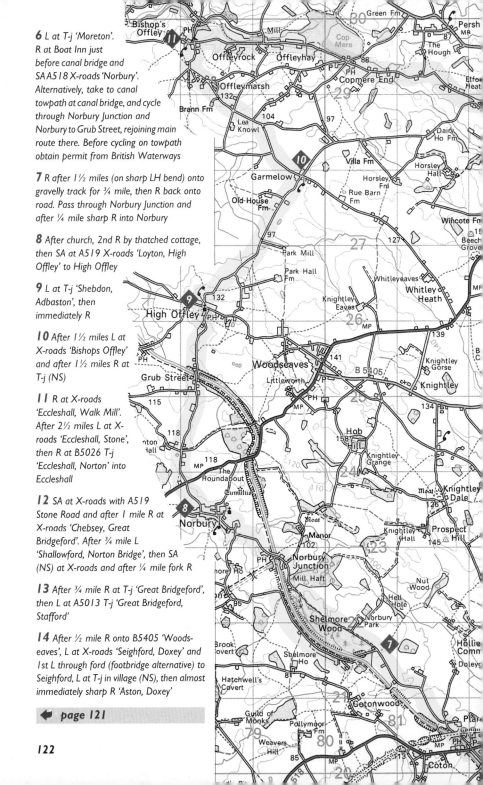

6 L at T-j 'Moreton'. R at Boat Inn just before canal bridge and SA A518 X-roads 'Norbury'. Alternatively, take to canal towpath at canal bridge, and cycle through Norbury Junction and Norbury to Grub Street, rejoining main route there. Before cycling on towpath obtain permit from British Waterways

7 R after 1½ miles (on sharp LH bend) onto gravelly track for ¾ mile, then R back onto road. Pass through Norbury Junction and after ¼ mile sharp R into Norbury

8 After church, 2nd R by thatched cottage, then SA at A519 X-roads 'Loyton, High Offley' to High Offley

9 L at T-j 'Shebdon, Adbaston', then immediately R

10 After 1½ miles L at X-roads 'Bishops Offley' and after 1½ miles R at T-j (NS)

11 R at X-roads 'Eccleshall, Walk Mill'. After 2½ miles L at X-roads 'Eccleshall, Stone', then R at B5026 T-j 'Eccleshall, Norton' into Eccleshall

12 SA at X-roads with A519 Stone Road and after 1 mile R at X-roads 'Chebsey, Great Bridgeford'. After ¾ mile L 'Shallowford, Norton Bridge', then SA (NS) at X-roads and after ¼ mile fork R

13 After ¾ mile R at T-j 'Great Bridgeford', then L at A5013 T-j 'Great Bridgeford, Stafford'

14 After ½ mile R onto B5405 'Woodseaves', L at X-roads 'Seighford, Doxey' and 1st L through ford (footbridge alternative) to Seighford, L at T-j in village (NS), then almost immediately sharp R 'Aston, Doxey'

← page 121

20 From Stafford through ancient Abbots Bromley returning via Cannock Chase or Shugborough Hall

Start

Stafford station

🅿 As above or in Castle Hill and Doxey Street, off ring road (free on Sundays and bank holidays)

Distance and grade

43 miles (short route 36)

 Easy/moderate

Terrain

Not very hilly, except for the climb from Blithfield reservoir to Abbots Bromley and up to Cannock Chase. The route is mainly on country lanes with only light traffic but the roads on the Chase can be busy (and attract speed merchants!)

Nearest railway

🚂 Stafford

🚉 INTERCITY: LONDON ► BIRMINGHAM ► NORTHWEST

🚉 LOCAL SERVICES: BIRMING-HAM ► WOLVERHAMPTON ► STOKE-ON-TRENT

🚂 Rugeley

🚉 STAFFORD ► LICHFIELD ► COVENTRY

A splendid route, deep into east Staffordshire, taking in the ancient town of Abbots Bromley, skirting remnants of Needham Forest near Hoar Cross and giving the option of an extended ride through the heaths and plantations of Cannock Chase.

```
128                    129
    Stafford
              Rugely
126        127
```

After the bustle of Stafford, red brick suburbia gives way to open views across the valley of the Sowe and a descent through pretty Tixall towards the Trent. There is a steep climb in Hixon but the route then keeps its height, with commanding views, until dropping to the causeway over Blithfield reservoir. After Abbots Bromley and Hoar Cross comes a series of peaceful villages, connected by minor roads, until a steep descent to Colton. Here there is a choice of returning directly to Stafford or taking a longer route over dramatic Cannock Chase.

 Stafford   Tixall   Hixon   Lea Heath   Admaston   Abbots Bromley   Hoar Cross

Places of interest

Tixall *2/3*
Only the gatehouse of the Hall survives but is still delightful and very impressive.

▲ *The Horn Dance at Abbots Bromley*

Abbots Bromley 7
The domestic architecture and scale give the town a tranquil and timeless quality – a good place to pause. Famous for the annual Horn Dance whose origins are lost in the pagan past when six Deer Men lead the dance; their horns (antlers) hang in church. The dance itself is on Monday following the first Sunday after September 4th. One mile after is Fishers Pit Rare Breeds Farm containing a collection of rare breeds of farm animals and wild fowl

Shugborough Hall 3
Neo-classical and set in sweeping parkland and gardens with a selection of 'Grecian' temples and follies. The interior is particularly noted for plasterwork by Vassall and Rose and there is also a working farm museum, the Staffordshire County Museum and a puppet museum. Access from Milford, or from Great Haywood is across the longest packhorse bridge in Britain

Refreshments

Canalside shop and teas, **Great Haywood**
Green Man PH, **Hixon**
Plenty of pubs in **Abbots Bromley**
Tearoom and picnic area, Fishers Pit Rare Breeds Farm (1 mile after **Abbots Bromley**)
Greyhound PH, **Colton**
Springslode Tea Bar, **Cannock Chase** (opposite Katyn Cemetery)
Barley Mow PH, **Milford**

rey Hamstall Ridware Blithbury Colton Rugeley Penkridge Bank Broadhurst Green Brocton Milford

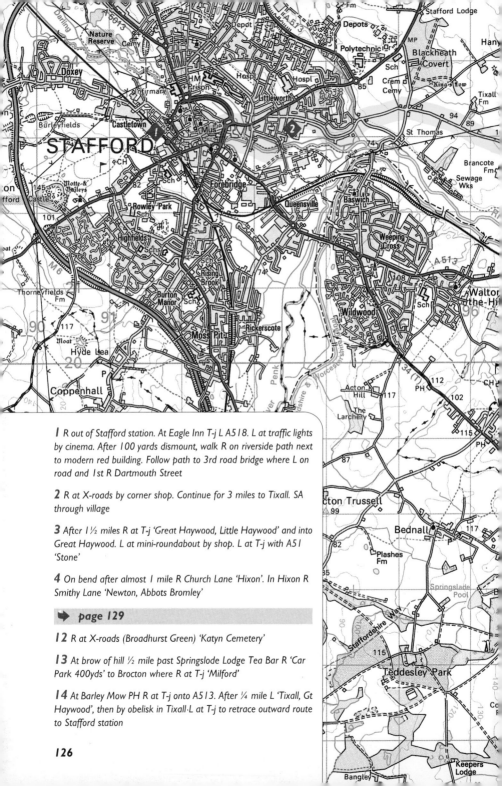

1 R out of Stafford station. At Eagle Inn T-j L A518. L at traffic lights by cinema. After 100 yards dismount, walk R on riverside path next to modern red building. Follow path to 3rd road bridge where L on road and 1st R Dartmouth Street

2 R at X-roads by corner shop. Continue for 3 miles to Tixall. SA through village

3 After 1½ miles R at T-j 'Great Haywood, Little Haywood' and into Great Haywood. L at mini-roundabout by shop. L at T-j with A51 'Stone'

4 On bend after almost 1 mile R Church Lane 'Hixon'. In Hixon R Smithy Lane 'Newton, Abbots Bromley'

➡ **page 129**

12 R at X-roads (Broadhurst Green) 'Katyn Cemetery'

13 At brow of hill ½ mile past Springslode Lodge Tea Bar R 'Car Park 400yds' to Brocton where R at T-j 'Milford'

14 At Barley Mow PH R at T-j onto A513. After ¼ mile L 'Tixall, Gt Haywood', then by obelisk in Tixall·L at T-j to retrace outward route to Stafford station

Short route

At instruction 10, in Colton, R at T-j with B5013 'Abbots Bromley, Uttoxeter'. After ¼ mile L 'Bishton, Stafford'. R at T-j with A51 'Stone' into Colwich, then L into village after ½ mile 'Little Haywood, Great Haywood'. Into and through Little Haywood and L at offset X-roads Mill Lane after RH bend in Great Haywood to retrace outward route to Stafford station

4 On bend after almost 1 mile R Church Lane 'Hixon'. In Hixon R Smithy Lane 'Newton, Abbots Bromley'

5 R at T-j in Lea Heath 'Adbaston, Abbots Bromley'. After 3½ miles L at T-j with B5013 up to Admaston. Over hill, down and across reservoir

6 Immediately R through car park and along shore. Bear L after 1 mile

7 In Abbots Bromley R Bagot Street at T-j and through town. After Coach and Horses PH L (B5234) 'Hoar Cross', then after 1 mile R 'Hoar Cross'

8 In Hoar Cross R 'Yoxall, Hoar Cross Hall', then after 1½ miles fork R 'Morrey, Hamstall Ridgware'

9 R at T-j after Morrey 'Hamstall Ridgware, Rugeley', then in Hamstall R at T-j 'Blithbury, Colton' and in Blithbury SA at offset X-roads by Bull and Spectacles PH

10 L at T-j with B5013 in Colton for longer route over Cannock Chase and R at T-j in 1½ miles under railway 'Rugeley' into town

11 At roundabout SA Anson Street 'Town Centre'. After a few hundred yards, opposite Market Hall ramp, R Crossley Stone. At T-j dismount to cross A51 then SA into Hagley Road and follow for 5 miles up into Cannock Chase

← **page 126**

21 From Great Wyrley through old mining areas, across upland heaths and forests

The first part of the route is through former mining villages in the South Staffordshire coalfield, then along progressively quieter country lanes in mixed farming land with views of Cannock Chase to the north. Shortly after reaching the Chase, the route goes off-road across heathland in the beautiful Sherbrook Valley, then after a short on-road stretch comes another off-road track through forest. Back on road you skirt the east side of the Chase through hilly and wooded villages and reach Castle Ring Iron Age hill fort and vantage point. A stretch through more former mining villages and then along narrow country lanes brings the rider back to the starting point. The route is suitable for both mountain bicycles and road bicycles. The two brief bridleway sections provide a good introduction to off-road cycling, totalling about 2 miles. Cyclists should give way to walkers and obey 'Danger: Forest Operations' signs.

Start

Landywood station

P As above and on adjoining roads. There is also a public car park to the east of the station
Alternative start from Lichfield – see directions

Distance and grade

25 miles

Moderate/strenuous

Terrain

There are no tremendous hills on the route but it is fairly strenuous on account of the hilly nature of much of the area, especially the eastern edge of the Chase. However as a reward there are good views in most directions and frequent points at which refreshments can be taken

Landywood station

Four Crosses

Broadhurst Green

Slitting M

🚉 Landywood
🚉 Hednesford
🚆 BIRMINGHAM ▶ WALSALL ▶
HEDNESFORD

🚉 Rugeley 🚆 STAFFORD ▶
LICHFIELD ▶ COVENTRY

Refreshments

Snacks and hot drinks at **Springslade Lodge Café**
Horns PH, **Slitting Mill**
Chetwynd Arms PH, **Upper Longdon**
Village stores, Park Gate Inn PH, **Cannock Wood**
Village stores, **Rawnsley**
Trafalgar PH, **Littleworth**

```
134        135
       ┌─────
      Lichfield
  Cannock
132        133
```

Places of interest

Cannock Chase 7 to 14
This is the smallest Area of Outstanding Natural Beauty in mainland Britain and the nearest to the West Midlands conurbation. One of the first areas selected by the Forestry Commission in 1920 for tree-planting, today much of it is covered by pine plantations. Specific features encountered on the route, or accessible via short detours, include:

Katyn Memorial In memory of Polish victims of a Second World War massacre

Marquis Drive Visitor Centre, Cannock Chase Country Park exhibition, information leaflets, maps and souvenirs

Forest Centre, Birches Valley Road forestry and wildlife displays and outdoor seating area

Castle Ring Iron Age Hill Fort, Cannock Wood defensive ramparts and ditches covering 10 acres. At 795 feet (242 m) above sea level it is the highest point of Cannock Chase and commands fine views. Please do not cycle on the fort area itself as this causes erosion problems

Forest of Mercia Project
All of the route south of the Chase falls within this project area. One future aim is to give a more wooded character to the landscape between the Black Country and Cannock Chase

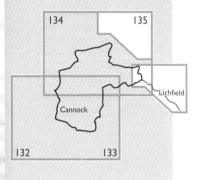

Upper Longdon   Cannock Wood   Rawnsley   Wimblebury

1 Leave Landywood station R up Streets Lane and L at T-j into Landywood Lane (NS). After ½ mile, in Cheslyn Hay, bear R (NS)

2 L along High Street at T-j. Bear R, then fork L 'Leisure Centre'. SA at A460 X-roads 'Calf Heath' **take care**

3 After 1 mile bear R and immediately R again 'Four Crosses, Hatherton'. R at T-j (NS), then L into Catsbridge Lane and R at T-j (NS)

4 At A5 X-roads SA 'Hatherton, Huntington' **take care**. After 200 yards bear L at Hatherton church

5 After ¾ mile L (NS) at end of row of houses, then SA after ¼ mile, ignoring fork L

6 R at T-j (NS), then bear L (NS) and SA at X-roads 'Pottalpool, Mansty' **take care**. After 1¼ miles R at X-roads 'Cannock, Stafford'

➡ **page 134**

14 L into Littleworth Road 'Hednesford, Cannock' and after ¾ miles L 'Heath Hayes, Norton Canes, Pelsall' (at this point SA, then 1st R and SA at X-roads with A460 for Hednesford station)

15 SA at roundabout B4154 'Norton Canes', R after 160 yards **easy to miss**, then immediately L and bear R into narrow lane. After ¾ mile R at T-j (NS), then fork L (NS) to A5

16 L at T-j A5 and R after 160 yards Gains Lane 'Little Wyrley'. **Take care** A5 is a very busy road – often safest to walk bicycles across. R at T-j (NS), then SA at X-roads (NS), SA at A34 offset X-roads into Bentons Lane **take care** , T-j R 'Station', then bear L to Landywood station

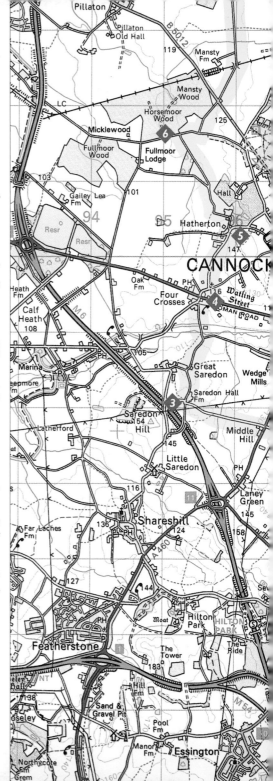

6 R at T-j (NS), then bear L (NS) and SA at X-roads 'Pottalpool, Mansty' **take care**. After 1¼ miles R at X-roads 'Cannock, Stafford'

7 SA at A34 X-roads 'Rugeley' **take care**, then L after 1 mile at X-roads 'Brocton'

8 After ¾ mile R at X-roads with gravel track 'Katyn Memorial' **easy to miss**. Continue along track with memorial on LH side, then SA through gate and along bridleway. SA through another gate and down into the Sherbrook Valley – **take care** on the loose gravel surface. At valley bottom SA 'Whitehouse'. Keep SA, ignoring tracks to R, then L to reach metalled road. L along metalled road. (**not** sharp L 'Rugeley Ranges')

9 2nd R after 1¾ miles Post Office Lane and R at T-j (NS). R at A460 T-j **take care**

10 After ½ mile L at X-roads with bridleway (just before a bus stop on LH side of road) **easy to miss**. Follow bridleway, ignoring two R forks. After ¼ mile track bears L, then R at top of hill. Continue SA through gate to Stile Cop Road. R, then immediately SA at X-roads Startly Lane 'Upper Longdon, Lichfield'.

11 In village, 4th R Huntsmans Hill, L at bottom of hill and immediately R into Bardy Lane. (3rd L for route back to Lichfield)

12 After 2½ miles R 'Beaudesert, Cannock Wood, Hednesford', then SA at X-roads into one-way street (NS). Continue SA to Castle Ring. From Castle Ring car park L down Holly Hill and bear R

13 At T-j R (NS), R into New Hayes Road 'Rawnsley, Hednesford', then R at T-j (NS)

14 L into Littleworth Road 'Hednesford, Cannock' and after ¾ miles L 'Heath Hayes, Norton Canes, Pelsall' (at this point SA, then 1st R and SA at X-roads with A460 for Hednesford station)

← page 132

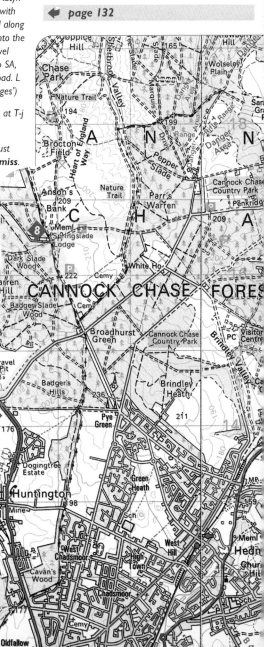

From Lichfield City station

R along A5127 to traffic lights, where L St John Street, then SA Bird Street (one-way, semi-pedestrianised) becoming Beacon Street. At roundabout SA Stafford Road to edge of city, L at T-j, then L again at traffic lights (A51) and almost immediately R to Farewell. R at T-j in Farewell then 1st L towards Upper Longdon to join main route at T-j between instructions 11 and 12

22 From Burton across Needwood to Uttoxeter, returning along the Dove Valley

Start

Burton-on-Trent station

P Off Station Street

Distance and grade

40 miles
Easy/moderate

A modest distance for a gentle day's ride, offering time to visit Sudbury Hall or linger over quiet lanes and villages. The route rapidly gains height out of Burton upon Trent, crossing the timeless farming uplands of ancient Needwood, then above the steep wooded banks from Draycott to Bagot Forest. There is a dramatic descent through Forest Banks down to Marchington Woodlands, then across changing levels until the roofs of Uttoxeter can be seen below. From Uttoxeter back to Burton upon Trent the route lies above the flood plain of the River Dove, through pleasantly preserved Marchington to Sudbury with its hall and at last to the ancient town of Tutbury with its castle.

Terrain

The route is for the most part fairly level, across upland or valley bottom. There are climbs from the Trent Valley to the upland above Burton upon Trent and from the Dove at Tutbury

Nearest railway

Burton-on-Trent
INTERCITY, REGIONAL RAILWAYS CENTRAL

Uttoxeter

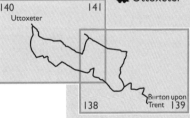

Places of interest

Burton upon Trent 1

A beery town. 'Oh, why was Burton built on Trent?' asked AE Housman, and you may smell the answer. The home of Bass, who have a Museum of Brewing, and Marstons, who still keep up the traditional 'Burton Union' method of brewing by continuous fermentation. The tradition was established by medieval monks, who found that the local well water was ideal for making beers and ales

Refreshments

Roebuck PH, **Burton upon Trent**
Bell PH, **Anslow**
Cock Inn, **Hanbury**
Bulls Head PH, Dog and Partridge PH, **Marchington**
Teashop and pubs, **Uttoxeter**
Vernon Arms PH, **Sudbury**
Tea room, **Sudbury Hall** Fosters Arms PH, **Scropton**
Leopard PH, **Tutbury** (in the shadow of the castle in Duke Street)

Uttoxeter 7

The centre of the town consists of irregular shaped market squares, one retaining its weighing machine from 1854

Tutbury 10

The town carries all the hallmarks of English history: Norman castle and church, the scars of Civil War and a main street of Tudor, Georgian and Regency buildings. There are glass works and antique shops which are worth visiting. The castle, with a commanding position overlooking the Dove and the town, has belonged to the Duchy of Lancaster since 1265

▼ The River Dove

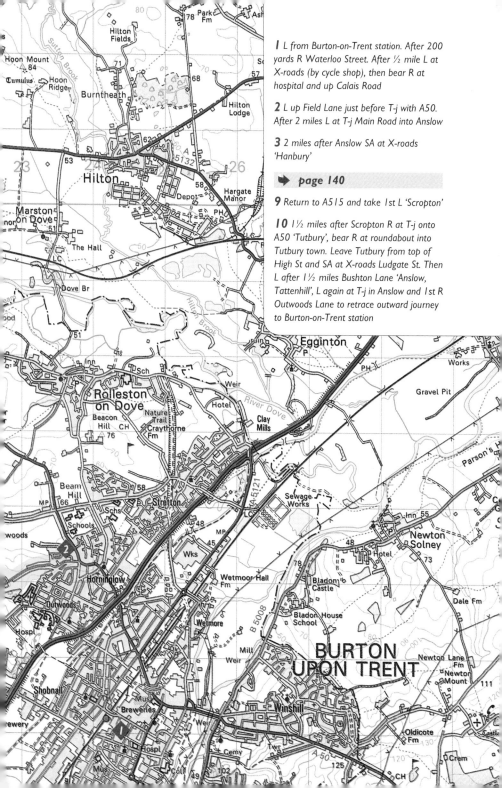

1 L from Burton-on-Trent station. After 200 yards R Waterloo Street. After ½ mile L at X-roads (by cycle shop), then bear R at hospital and up Calais Road

2 L up Field Lane just before T-j with A50. After 2 miles L at T-j Main Road into Anslow

3 2 miles after Anslow SA at X-roads 'Hanbury'

➨ **page 140**

9 Return to A515 and take 1st L 'Scropton'

10 1½ miles after Scropton R at T-j onto A50 'Tutbury', bear R at roundabout into Tutbury town. Leave Tutbury from top of High St and SA at X-roads Ludgate St. Then L after 1½ miles Bushton Lane 'Anslow, Tattenhill', L again at T-j in Anslow and 1st R Outwoods Lane to retrace outward journey to Burton-on-Trent station

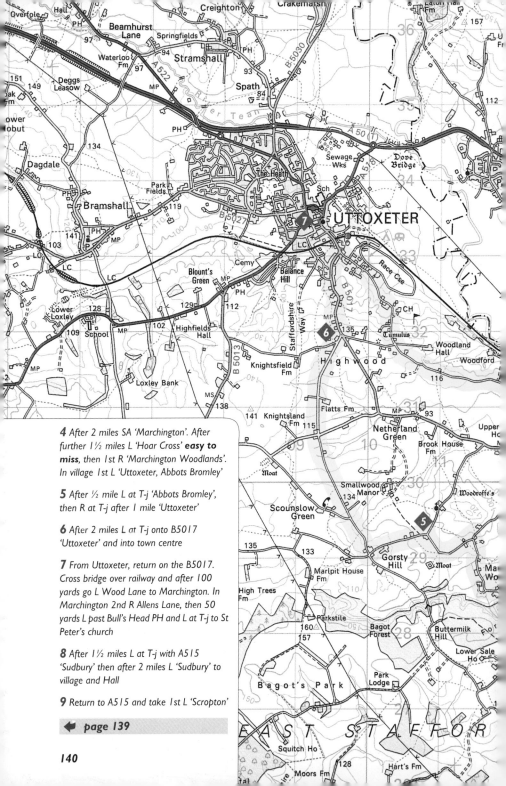

4 After 2 miles SA 'Marchington'. After further 1½ miles L 'Hoar Cross' **easy to miss**, then 1st R 'Marchington Woodlands'. In village 1st L 'Uttoxeter, Abbots Bromley'

5 After ½ mile L at T-j 'Abbots Bromley', then R at T-j after 1 mile 'Uttoxeter'

6 After 2 miles L at T-j onto B5017 'Uttoxeter' and into town centre

7 From Uttoxeter, return on the B5017. Cross bridge over railway and after 100 yards go L Wood Lane to Marchington. In Marchington 2nd R Allens Lane, then 50 yards L past Bull's Head PH and L at T-j to St Peter's church

8 After 1½ miles L at T-j with A515 'Sudbury' then after 2 miles L 'Sudbury' to village and Hall

9 Return to A515 and take 1st L 'Scropton'

◀ **page 139**

Cycle
TOURS

The Ordnance Survey Cycle Tours series

Around Birmingham
Avon, Somerset & Wiltshire
Berks, Bucks & Oxfordshire
Cornwall & Devon
Cumbria & the Lakes
Dorset, Hampshire & Isle of Wight
East Anglia – South
Gloucestershire and Hereford & Worcester
Kent, Surrey & Sussex
Southern Scotland

The whole series is available from all good bookshops or by mail order direct from the publisher. Payment can be made by credit card or cheque/postal order in the following ways

By phone

Phone through your order on our special *Credit Card Hotline* on *01933 414000.* Speak to our customer service team during office hours (9am to 5pm) or leave a message on the answer machine, quoting your full credit card number plus expiry date, your full name and address and reference T503N73C

By post

Simply fill out the order form opposite and send it to:
Cash Sales Department, Reed Book Services, PO Box 5, Rushden, Northants, NN10 6YX

Cycle TOURS

I wish to order the following titles

	Price	Quantity	Total
Around Birmingham ISBN 0 600 58623 5	£9.99		
Avon, Somerset & Wiltshire ISBN 0 600 58664 2	£9.99		
Berks, Bucks & Oxfordshire ISBN 0 600 58156 X	£9.99		
Cornwall & Devon ISBN 0 600 58124 1	£9.99		
Cumbria & the Lakes ISBN 0 600 58126 8	£9.99		
Dorset, Hampshire & Isle of Wight ISBN 0 600 58667 7	£9.99		
East Anglia – South ISBN 0 600 58125 X	£9.99		
Gloucestershire and Hereford & Worcester ISBN 0 600 58665 0	£9.99		
Kent, Surrey & Sussex ISBN 0 600 58666 9	£9.99		
Southern Scotland ISBN 0 600 58624 3	£9.99		

Postage and packing free   Grand total

Name _____ (block capitals)

Address _____

_____ Postcode

I enclose a cheque/postal order for £ [   ] made payable to **Reed Book Services Ltd**

or please debit my ☐ Access ☐ Visa ☐ American Express ☐ Diners account

number [ ][ ][ ][ ] [ ][ ][ ][ ] [ ][ ][ ][ ] [ ][ ][ ][ ]

by £ [   ]   expiry date [ ][ ][ ]   _____ Signature